I0012267

simplicity

sustainable,
humane,
and effective
software development

dave thomas

The Pragmatic Bookshelf

Dallas, Texas

See our complete catalog of hands-on, practical,
and Pragmatic content for software developers:
https://pragprog.com

Sales, volume licensing, and support:
support@pragprog.com

Derivative works, AI training and testing,
international translations, and other rights:
rights@pragprog.com

The team that produced this book includes:

Publisher: Dave Thomas
COO: Janet Furlow
Development Editor: Susannah Davidson
Copy Editor: L. Sakhi MacMillan
Indexing: Potomac Indexing, LLC

Copyright © 2025 David Thomas.

All rights reserved. No part of this publication may be reproduced by any means, nor may any derivative works be made from this publication, nor may this content be used to train or test an artificial intelligence system, without the prior consent of the publisher.

When we are aware that a term used in this book is claimed as a trademark, the designation is printed with an initial capital letter or in all capitals.

The Pragmatic Starter Kit, The Pragmatic Programmer, Pragmatic Programming, Pragmatic Bookshelf, PragProg, and the linking *g* device are trademarks of The Pragmatic Programmers, LLC.

Every precaution was taken in the preparation of this book. However, the publisher assumes no responsibility for errors or omissions or for damages that may result from the use of information (including program listings) contained herein.

ISBN-13: 979-8-88865-154-4
Book version: P1.0—June 2025

You must either make a tool of the creature, or a man of him. You cannot make both. Men were not intended to work with the accuracy of tools, to be precise and perfect in all their actions. If you will have that precision out of them, and make their fingers measure degrees like cog-wheels, and their arms strike curves like compasses, you must unhumanize them. All the energy of their spirits must be given to make cogs and compasses of themselves....

On the other hand, if you will make a man of the working creature, you cannot make him a tool. Let him but begin to imagine, to think, to try to do anything worth doing; and the engine-turned precision is lost at once. Out come all his roughness, all his dullness, all his incapability; shame upon shame, failure upon failure, pause after pause: but out comes the whole majesty of him also; and we know the height of it only when we see the clouds settling upon him.

John Ruskin, *The Stones of Venice*

Contents

Part I — Simplify What You Do
Simplify How You Do It

Part II — Simplify Your Environment

Part III — Simplify Your Interactions

Part IV — Simplify Your Code

Let's Change Our World—Again

Software development is inherently complex.

Unfortunately, we seem to delight in making it not just complex but complicated too.

What's the difference? A snowflake is complex; the weather system that produced it is complicated. Both have many parts, but with the snowflake you can see how they interact—you'll find a pattern, and some rules.

With software, complexity is difficult, but it has rules. Complications arise when we don't follow them. And these complications turn our projects into hard-to-understand, hard-to-predict, tangled balls of logic. They interfere with the way we run our projects, and the way we deal with people.

Working with complications is like playing a game where not only do you not know the rules but you can't know the rules.

The sad thing? Most of the complications in our projects are self-induced. We add them when we don't stop to think, when we don't take the time to listen to that small inner voice saying "really?"

We don't invest the time to make things simple, because we have no time. We have no time because things are complicated.

We have to make the time; if we don't, we won't learn and improve. We have to discover how to embrace simplicity and create simple things, otherwise we'll spend our time like the plate juggler, running between the poles to stop things from crashing down.

Ward Cunningham coined the phrase, "Do the simplest thing that could possibly work." That's not just a way of writing code; it applies to everything we do.

Simplicity doesn't mean simplistic. It doesn't mean naïve. It means producing things that are easy to understand and change, and that have that vague quality of "feeling right." Christopher Alexander, the architect who wrote the original *A Pattern Language: Towns, Buildings, Construction [AIS77]*, called this the *quality without a name*. Achieving simplicity rewards you with this feeling.

Don't Do What I Do

A problem writing about simplicity is that no rules or procedures exist that make things simple, no coding standards or design methodologies that guarantee the things you produce will not end up complicated. Simplicity isn't the way you do things; it's the spirit with which you do them.

Why? Because what's simple to me might not seem so to you, and something you find simple might go over my head.

I cannot tell you what to do, because I don't know. I can't give you a structured set of rules to follow, because there aren't any. Instead, I decided to teach by example. I divided the book into a set of *practices*. Each is motivated by a situation that I've been in that felt more complex than it should. For each, I outline the steps I took to simplify things.

What I did is not any kind of general-purpose solution to the problem; I don't want you to copy my steps unthinkingly. Instead, I hope that you'll read each practice as a kind of story—the path I took to make something simpler. Treat this as an example as you find your own path.

Courage

Kent Beck kicked off modern software development with *Extreme Programming Explained: Embrace Change [Bec00]*. He lists the five values of XP as Communication, Feedback, Respect, Simplicity, and Courage. I believe these are core values not just for Extreme Programming, not just for programming in general, but for life.

Ultimately the ideas in this book all make great demands on you as a person. They ask you to create and follow a set of values, often in the face of peer pressure. They ask you to think about what you're doing rather than going with the flow, and they inform you when you have to make a stand. And they ask you to fight against all the factors that make things complex as you try to bring simplicity into your life.

All this takes courage. All great changes do.

Enjoy the process.

See You Online

https://pragprog.com/titles/dtcode
> The book's home page, with links to its discussion forum and the errata list.

https://articles.pragdave.me
> Where I write articles and notes about simplicity and whatever else catches my fancy.

https://pragdave.me
> My personal home page.

https://pragprog.com
> My business and the last 20 years of my life.

My Thanks

To my reviewers: Aino Corry, Bruce Eckel, Derek Sivers, Kim Shrier, Neal Ford, Noel Rappin, Saron Yitbarek, and Zachary McKenna. True friends are the people who tell you you're wrong without making you feel like a complete fool.

To my editor: this is the first time in 25 years of writing books that I've had an editor, and I'm never going back. Susannah Davidson is incredibly skilled at seeing the big picture and the small details, all at the same time, and finding ways to make them coherent. Another friend.

To my wife: for being my wife *and* my friend.

And, finally, to all of you, for listening.

## CHAPTER 1

An Approach to Simplicity

I can't tell you how to do things with simplicity; everyone's context is different.

Instead, I'm going to describe a bunch of situations which are crying out to be simplified, and then we're going to look at what I did to simplify them.

I'm not doing this to show off, or so that you can copy me. My goal here is to show you an approach you can use to recognize and cut away complexity. I call it Orient, Step, Learn.

Orient, Step, Learn

Scientists and engineers spend their lives exploring unknowns. For at least 400 years, the approach they've chosen has been largely unchanged:

- Come up with a hypothesis.
- Design an experiment to try to disprove it.
- Analyze the results and repeat.

This is the essence of the *scientific method.*

We can follow the same approach when we approach complexity.

Orient

> We need to discover something we feel is too complex. This process can be obvious: no one knows how this code works. It can be subtle: that nagging intuition that gives you pause.

> When this happens, we stop and think. What are the approaches we could take to make things simpler. And, most importantly, how will we know whether the result actually is simpler?

> Do this over time, and you'll develop a spidey-sense, that indefinable feeling that warns you that something isn't how it should be.

Take a Step

The key concept here is the word "step." We don't plan a journey; we don't write a set of procedures; we don't abandon what we were doing.

Instead we find the simplest thing we could do that tests out our idea. The less time and effort it takes, the faster we can decide whether to pursue it or drop it. If we were wrong, it hasn't cost us a lot.

Learn

The step is complete; the experiment is over. Now's the time to reflect. One step is rarely enough, so it's vital to use the information you learn from prior steps to inform each subsequent one.

All the sections in the rest of the book are called *practices*, because they represent things you have to practice if they are to become second nature. The more you make yourself orient (recognize complexity), step (try an experiment), and learn (adjust what you do), the less you'll have to remember to do it going forward. It'll be just like driving: something you do without having to think which pedal does what.

Maybe write "Orient, Step, Learn" on an index card and tape it where you can see it while you work. If you work alone (or with understanding people), it actually helps to say each step out loud as you do it. The more stimuli you give your brain, the quicker it becomes an innate pattern.

Anyway, onward!

Part I

Simplify What You Do
Simplify How You Do It

## CHAPTER 2

Lose Weight Now...

Studies going back almost 100 years show that when you expand a road network by $x\%$, traffic inevitably grows by at least $x\%$. Economists call this *induced demand*: when there's more of something, people will use it.

At college, my department ran an IBM/370-135. It supported 20 simultaneous online users, most doing development work. It had a total of 384 kB of memory. Nowadays, you'd be lucky to fit a single web app into 1,000 times that space.

We can boast that the phone in our pocket has more GFlops than the entire world's hardware in 1970, but we forget that they put people on the moon using a flight guidance computer with 4 kB of RAM and less than 40 kB of storage, all clocked at a whopping 2 MHz.

Thanks to Moore's Law, we don't particularly care; we have our own kind of induced demand. It's an unwritten rule of development: there are always more gigahertz and gigabytes—have fun.

But this expansion comes with a number of costs. Let's ignore the environmental and resource-depletion issues and selfishly look at our parochial world of writing software.

Our code is becoming more and more bloated. That makes it harder to understand, harder to maintain, and (as we'll see) harder to deploy in the future.

It's time to make our code healthier—it's time to put it on a diet.

Cut Back on Unhealthy Dependencies

It's late 2024. I just created a new Phoenix project using mix phx.new my_project. It had 43 dependencies, which came in at 15 MB.

A new Rails project installs 83 gems, and these in turn load hundreds more. Here's a dependency graph of a basic Rails app.

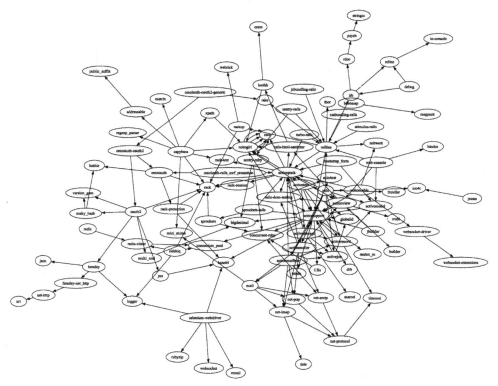

npx create-react-app my-app downloaded 874 modules (about 350 MB of code) for a basic React app. I had time to make a cup of tea.

I'm not claiming that React is bloated compared to the others. I'm saying that they *all* are carrying around a lot of baggage. And these are the numbers for baseline, empty projects. As you start adding code, you'll be adding dependencies of your own (and those dependencies will have their own dependencies, and so on).

I hate dependencies—every last one of them.

Every dependency I use gives control of a part of my future to a tree of third parties, people I probably don't know, can't control, and in reality can't even trust. Probably tens of thousands of people have contributed to the 874 modules that React uses out of the box. It only takes one of them to break my app.

Idea 1	Every dependency gives away control of part of your app

In March 2016, a prolific developer of JavaScript libraries suddenly removed all of them from the NPM repository. Among these modules was one named left-pad which, not surprisingly, added padding characters to the start of a string until it reached a given length.

The left-pad library was used by many thousands of other libraries, and these in turn by even more libraries. These second-order libraries included mainstays of the JavaScript world, such as Babel and React.

One developer's decision rendered a significant proportion of JavaScript apps unbuildable.

In March 2024, a global warning (CVE-2024-3094) was issued after malicious code was found embedded in the XZ compression library. This was particularly concerning because the library was used by the OpenSSH daemon code, potentially compromising what was assumed to be a secure data transport.

When you add a dependency to your code, you're inviting a bunch of developers into your project, giving them access to your runtime. And these developers don't have to be malicious to cause problems: they can change APIs, deprecate features, or accidentally add security vulnerabilities.

My Personal Dependency Hell

In 2023 I came back to the Pragmatic Bookshelf after a seven-year break only to discover that the software that was the backbone of our business had effectively been unmaintained. It was still running Rails 3 (Rails is currently at version 8).

No problem, I thought, I'll migrate it up to the latest Rails, one release at a time.

Except Rails 3 uses a library that used a library that...was totally different on modern machines. I couldn't even build the Rails 3 gems. I tried just updating blindly, only to discover that Rails had so many breaking changes between all these releases that I couldn't even get the app to start.

In the end, the only thing I could do was create a Docker container running an eight-year-old version of Linux that still had the old libraries. After a frustrating week, I finally had the most complex (and fragile) development environment I've ever used. I'm still managing the fallout as we migrate away.

Simplifying Dependencies

Remember the left-pad fiasco? Here's the entire code from the library:

```
module.exports = leftpad;
function leftpad (str, len, ch) {
  str = String(str);
  var i = -1;
  if (!ch && ch !== 0) ch = ' ';
  len = len - str.length;
  while (++i < len) {
    str = ch + str;
  }
  return str;
}
```

It's 11 lines of fairly ugly code; the line str = ch + str gives me garbage-collection nightmares.

Somewhere out there are developers who thought, "I need to left-pad this string" and who then took the time to search for a library, add it to their build, and work out how to import and use it. It probably took them three times as long as it would have done to write it themselves.

Today, padstart is built into JavaScript. Even if it weren't, a decent implementation could be just three lines of code:

```
function leftpad (str, len, ch=" ") {
    str = String(str);
    len = len - str.length;
    return (len > 0) ? ch.repeat(len) + str : str;
}
```

Idea 2	**Eleven lines of code should not be a dependency**

I know—this is an extreme case. But it's still useful to think about why folks chose to find a library for something so trivial. They probably were under time constraints, although in this case finding the library probably took longer than writing the code.

They may also have fallen into the *someone-else's-problem* trap. Delegating code to the author of a library means that they're not responsible for any problems.

Obviously I need to add dependencies to my project; I'm not going to write an SSH library from scratch—that would be ridiculous. But there's a trade-off to be made: adding a dependency today may solve a problem today. At the same time, it adds complexity for future-me in terms of risk and maintenance.

Isolating Dependencies

In the past, I've been bitten when a dependency that I've used extensively in an app suddenly changed an API; I'd have to update code across multiple source files to adapt to that change.

Now, if possible, whenever I use a dependency widely in an app, I wrap it in a simple function and use that function in the rest of the code. That way, if the API changes, I might be able to get away with updating just the wrapper function.

The Dependency Decision Chain

Before adding a dependency to a project, I consider:

Do I need the functionality?

Younger Dave often added a new dependency after I read about some cool new feature online. I did it because it looked interesting, not because my project absolutely needed it.

Now I try to have the discipline not to experiment like that; if my project will work without it, I won't add it. Remember that "less is more." (Of course, nothing stops me from playing around with it in my spare time...)

Is it easier just to code it?

Increasingly, I find myself not using dependencies if all I need from them is a single function. If I can write it myself, I do. If the library is open source and the license permits, I might copy the function (with attribution) into my own code, where I can examine it and possibly update it to fit the project's needs better.

Am I buying a jungle?

Joe Armstrong said about dependencies, "You wanted a banana but what you got was a gorilla holding the banana and the entire jungle." Sometimes the functionality I want comes with a lot of baggage. Maybe I just need to escape HTML strings, but the library I found contains an entire HTML parsing and creation system along with a dozen external dependencies for things like lexing, indentation, and so on.

All that extra cruft is a liability. I may not be using it, but it still contributes to the code that I might be fighting with in the future.

Is this vital to my project?

If so, I'd better make sure I have a local copy. Nothing's quite like the sinking feeling of getting a 404 when you try to fetch something your project needs.

Am I locked to a particular version?

I always use a dependency manager for the libraries I use. I also use one (currently asdf) for the tools. These allow me to specify the versions of everything I use when creating a project.

That's fine for a while, but eventually there'll come a day when I try to add one more dependency, and it relies on a newer version of some dependency I already have. I update that dependency but then break the dependency requirements for five more libraries. Sometimes the most innocuous addition can end up causing an update that ripples through half my dependencies. And when I make those updates, I'm hoping that my tests will cover the obscure corner cases that might break.

During development, I got into the habit of updating my dependencies daily or weekly, banking on the idea that smaller steps will be easier to handle. But this doesn't help down the road, after I've moved on. When I come back to a project after only a year or so, I assume I'm going to be battling with dependencies for a while before I can start being productive.

And because dependencies depend on each other, too, each additional dependency will cost you more than a linear amount of time down the road.

Am I secure?

Many library repositories monitor for reported security vulnerabilities in the libraries they host. When you install a JavaScript library using NPM, for example, it will perform a quick audit of all your packages, and not just the ones you're installing:

```
$ npm add jest
npm warn deprecated glob@7.2.3: Glob versions prior to v9 are no longer supported
added 275 packages, and audited 310 packages in 13s
33 vulnerabilities (6 moderate, 19 high, 8 critical)
Run `npm audit` for details.
```

In this example, the deprecation warning is caused by adding Jest, but the 33 vulnerabilities were all in existing packages.

During development, I see these reports whenever I refresh my dependencies. After that time, I get warnings from GitHub if it notices a security issue in my codebase.

Idea 3	**Make each dependency a deliberate choice**

Here's what I currently do:

- I don't use a whole dependency for just a single function.
- I don't use a dependency for something I could simply write.
- I try to keep dependencies updated during development.
- I spend a little time checking the provenance of dependencies before adding them.

Here's what I should get better at doing:

- Investigate services which monitor the security status of dependencies.
- Get more consistent about wrapping dependencies to isolate them from the rest of my code.
- Set aside a day a quarter to fetch and build old projects, updating their dependencies if possible.

Your checklists will be different. But having your own deliberate decision-making process will help you to weight the benefits of each dependency you add.

Investigate

Open up your current project and have a look at all the top-level dependencies (the ones you and your team have declared).

- Do you know what each does?
- Do you know how your code is using each? Is that use trivial? Can you remove the dependency and simply implement the functionality you were using?

Now look at the list of all the dependencies (not just the ones you explicitly included). These will typically be in something like a .lock file.

- How many are there?
- Does that number scare you?
- Are you going to do something about it?

Frameworks: Read the Ingredients

These days, I'd guess a majority of projects run inside some kind of framework. That's good: frameworks handle the low-level details and let you get on with writing application-level code. Frameworks should make your code simpler. Sometimes, they do.

But other times, tying your codebase to a framework is like jumping on a runaway train—you move fast, but it's scary and there's likely to be a crash at some point.

Why am I so cynical?

Come Into My Parlor

A framework envelops your application code; it's in charge, and your code provides callbacks and hooks for it to call. When you need to get something done, you call out to the framework.

Once you've committed to a framework, you're not going to be able to extract your code without a whole lot of hassle. Not only does the framework control your APIs, it also defines how you architect your application.

This might be acceptable if the team in charge of the framework guarantees long-term stability. Most don't.

Inflation Spirals

Creating a new framework is a lot of work. Introducing it to the public, and handling all their questions, suggestions, and flames, is even more work. Learning to manage your contributors is taxing. And there's the day job, too.

So the people who succeed creating frameworks have to be passionate and driven.

Sometimes a framework will be the first in its field. If it's popular, competitors will appear, each claiming to do something better. The first framework responds, adding some of these new features, claiming to do them better still. Other frameworks then release their own new features.

Other times, the custodian of a framework realizes there's a better way to do something (or even just a sexy new way). If you're lucky, they'll deprecate the old way for a while before turning it off in favor of the new way.

And so we see frameworks constantly evolving, adding new features, and discarding older features that are no longer cool. ("You were using that? Well, you'll need to rewrite your code if you want to stay on the train.")

It's a very rare framework that doesn't get larger and more complex over time. The bigger the framework, the bigger (and more complex) your app, and the larger the number of dependencies you're carrying.

Idea 4	**Frameworks accrete functionality**

In fact, the dangers of complex frameworks can come at you in two ways.

Green Field Projects

Back when I was playing with full-stack JavaScript apps, I was constantly researching what was new and hot, looking for those groovy new features that would make me a cool kid. I reasoned that something new and popular *must* be better than the three-month-old framework I had been using.

I'd watch a couple of videos with surprisingly conflicting installation instructions, so I kind of went with both. It took three or four tries, but eventually the "Hello, World!" app starts up. From here on in, it's just a simple matter of implementation....

First up: handle an incoming request. But how? The framework has sync and async options. The async side can use callbacks or events, and you can add your own state machine for finer control. And there's the choice of messaging infrastructure; I could install any one of four options. Before doing any of this, I need to generate an SSL certificate, and the framework's brand-new security release insists on you giving it a valid Root certificate.

Idea 5	**If a framework gives you options,** **it contains things you don't need**

All these options and features come with a price—they add complexity, dependencies, and bloat. And unused functionality that's just sitting there could well be tomorrow's security hole.

Brown Field Projects

Maybe you've been using a framework since V0.8. You've grown up with it, and your team knows it well. Increasingly, though, the rate of change and deprecations has been bogging you down. You absolutely have to integrate new framework releases to get the security updates, but each release brings incompatibilities, which means you're spending your time updating existing code and not writing new code. Even worse, your team enjoys exploring new facets of the framework and are constantly changing code to use them, even when there's no apparent difference from the end-user's perspective.

Idea 6	**If you spend more time maintaining your framework than your code, maybe the framework's not helping**

When it was new and lean, that framework helped you deploy your new app in record time. But now that you depend on it, it seems to be slowing you down.

So, No Frameworks?

Of course, you should use frameworks. But here's my strong advice. Don't choose the framework with the most features and the newest technologies. It might be fun initially, but you may well regret it a year from now.

Instead, choose a framework that's been around—and stable—for a while. Choose a framework that has the fewest features that still does what you need it to do.

For example, if you're creating a server-side API in Ruby, look into something minimal, such as Sinatra, before you reach for Rails. In JavaScript, consider Express as well as Nest or Adonis.

The guiding principle here is that the better you understand your environment, the simpler it is to use. The smaller your environment, the easier it is to understand and maintain. It's also easier to bring new developers up to speed.

Remember, less is more when it comes to frameworks, too.

What's your FBQ (Framework Bloat Quotient)?

(This is a tongue-in-cheek rhetorical question, but it's still interesting to think about.)

Pick a framework you're currently using. Somewhere in its documentation will be a list of its features. What percentage of these are you using? When I've asked teams this question in the past, the most popular answers are in the 10%–20% range. If your number is similar, you're using the visible part of the iceberg.

The Best Features Are the Ones You Don't Ship

I can't help it. Just like the lab rat pushing the button to get the next food pellet, I love delivering features—creating and delivering something new. In the past, I was known for delivering features the customer didn't even know they wanted. That's a superhero play.

It's also ridiculously stupid.

Every feature we add to our software represents a future liability, because all that code will need to be supported, maintained, extended, and understood by new developers.

Idea 7	*Feature* is marketing speak for *future liability*

Does that stop everyone adding feature after feature? No.

Should it?

Yes, sometimes.

Need-Driven Development

A basic rule for keeping software simple is *Don't write code unless someone needs the functionality it provides.i* And "wouldn't it be cool if…" and "it'd be really easy to add…" don't count as need.

Idea 8	**Don't write code no one asked for**

Obviously, need depends on your context. If your company is creating a mass-market product, then the marketing folks will likely be keeping an eye on competitors and creating feature requests to keep up and surpass them. That's genuine need.

But if you're creating software for a single client or internal use, then the concept of need becomes more interesting. It can also be tainted by politics.

I've spoken to managers who have to budget for software development. Every year they prepare a report saying what they want to build, how much it will cost, and what value it will produce. They'll receive back an approval to spend some amount, normally lower than their request. So what do they do? They add all the features they think they might need to the project before they submit it. This both bumps up the budget and acts as a form of insurance; they don't want to ask for a baseline project this year only to get turned down for the extensions they need next year. This applies to both internal and external clients.

But we can be more agile than that. Back when I was delivering software to paying customers, I'd flip the equation around. Rather than talking about need, I'd ask the customer where they'd extract value from the project and what their priorities were for doing so.

| Idea 9 | **Deliver incremental value, not features** |

Then the team and I would go away and assign a level of effort to delivering these values. This is purely internal to the team; we just needed a sense of how big the task was. The result of the guess would be as simple as "easy," "medium," "difficult," and "unknown."

We'd take these rough estimates and compare them to the value they'd deliver. Assuming the dependencies would allow it, we could then work out which features we could deliver early that would also give the customer a decent amount of business value.

Then we'd go back to the customer and say something like this:

> We've been looking at your requirements, and we think we can give you some options. This first is a conventional project, where we deliver the software to you at the end.

> With the second option, we'll deliver the software incrementally, feature by feature. We looked through your list of values and combined them with our project planning, and we feel that we can deliver feature X well before the final project is complete. You should be able to start using it then, getting business value early. We can talk nearer the time about subsequent deliveries, but right now we think we might look at features Y and Z next.

This gives the customer two big wins. First, they can start earning some value from the software earlier; value now is always better than the same value later. Second, your customer gets to experience using this first deliverable. In my experience, when the customer first uses a partial delivery, they suddenly realize things about the system that weren't apparent when it was just some words in a document. They'll be able to come back to you with ideas and suggestions for next steps that might be radically different from their original request. In fact, a while back I had a customer who took the first two of five feature deliveries and then said the system did just what they needed; the extra three features were there for insurance, and they weren't required.

It also gives you some massive wins. First, you get feedback a lot earlier than you would have. Ideally you'll be talking with the customer every week, but often that just doesn't happen. But you'll definitely get their attention when you deliver something. Second, you start to build a trusting relationship with them. When the project started, they were taking a risk on you. When you deliver something, even if it's not the complete project, they'll start feeling a lot more comfortable, and you'll find that you'll get more open and useful interactions with them. Finally, this approach catches potential problems early: if you have a misunderstanding that would propagate throughout the code, finding out early stops a whole lot of rework later.

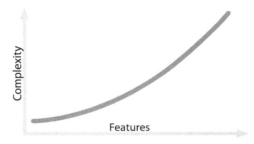

| Idea 10 | **Complexity grows faster than feature count** |

Simplicity

You can't ship software that does nothing. But you can work to reduce the number of features, delivering only what's needed, free from unnecessary embellishments or complications, and delivering it earlier. Features can always be added later.

Look back

Look back at some projects you've delivered. What percentage of the code in each gets used on a daily basis? What percentage would you guess never gets used?

## CHAPTER 3

Simplify Your Projects

So far, I've been looking at ways we can simplify our approach to the technologies we use. That's a good thing because that's where we have the most power to change things.

But I have to acknowledge that I'm in a privileged position: I work for myself, and the majority of code I write is in support of that business.

So when it came time to talk about projects and teams, I reached out. At the end of 2023 I opened up my calendar and invited teams to chat with me. Over the next few months I spoke with roughly 50 teams from around the world.

Two things surprised me. The first was how committed these people were to doing a good job. They were well aware of what was going well and what was going badly, and they often had plans to remediate their problems.

The second surprise was how often solutions to a particular problem arose independently; teams on different continents and in different cultures had solved a problem using the same techniques.

One question I asked was "Do you consider your team to be successful?" For those that did, I asked, "What do you think leads to that success?" Here are three areas they tended to mention:

Communication

Information travels through the team quickly and accurately.

Team members may not agree with each other, but they accept that others have points of views.

Complementary skills

Different people handle different tasks, with no task being more valued than another.

Generous with experience

> People view it as a responsibility to pass their knowledge and experience on to their teammates.

In this chapter, we'll explore these areas, channeling both my own experience and, more importantly, the experience of all these teams.

As always, this is what worked for me and for them. It might work for you, too, but don't just copy and hope. Assess and adapt.

Practice 4

Decouple Your Teams

Any organization that designs a system (broadly defined)
will produce a design that mirrors the organization's
communication structure.

> *Melvin Conway, 1968*

Over the years we developers have learned a few things about writing code. We've even developed a series of intuitions, like these:

- Decoupled code is easier to change.
- APIs and boundaries make code easier to ingest.
- Small chunks are easier to write than large ones.
- Layers of abstractions help tame complexity.

(Why *intuitions*? Some pundits have the hubris to say that they've developed *rules* or *laws* of coding. Ask them when they last wrote a decent-sized chunk o' code.)

So it seems obvious to ask if any of our intuitions about writing good code would let us simplify how projects are run.

I think we can extract some interesting insights by playing with this idea. Let's look at how we could apply decoupling to our teams.

Decoupling

Decoupling code is all about managing dependencies to limit the impact of change.

If two or more pieces of code are coupled, then a change to one might well break the others—no change is localized. Working with coupled code is a constant juggling act, and it's one where gravity always wins.

Team members can also be coupled in this way, and when one person depends on another, change becomes harder and takes longer. The more interdependencies, the more fragile the team.

We're not talking about the code they write here; we're talking about processes and practices. Coupling in this context is anything that forces multiple team members to wait on another team member. In *The Pragmatic Programmer, 20th Anniversary Edition [TH19]*, I called this *temporal coupling*.

> **Idea 11** **Coupling affects both teams and code**

Here are some examples of temporal coupling in teams:

- Team members work on a single feature at a time. When they are finished, they cannot proceed until someone else has reviewed their work.

- Hassan's code is dependent on Jan's code. Jan is on vacation, so Hassan cannot proceed.

- Jan calls an all-hands meeting at the last moment. People drop what they're doing only to end up discussing the selection of drinks in the vending machine. Everyone is coupled in time: for the length of the meeting nothing else happens. After the meeting, it takes 10 minutes for people to end their conversations and another 30 minutes to regroup and regain the context of what they were doing before the meeting.

- The team uses two-week sprints. Every two weeks, they deliver, have a retrospective, and do some backlog triage and some planning.

  The coupling involved in this is staggering. Individual features must be synchronized. New work may get stopped until the start of the next sprint. Everyone drops everything for the chain of meetings. And any problems cause the whole team to spin.

The Async Life

Too many teams are event driven: if something comes along, you're expected to drop what you're doing to deal with it. Then you have to get two other people involved, and the rift in concentration spreads like cracks on thin ice.

In his review of a draft of this book, Noel Rappin raised an interesting point:

> I've been on teams that called this "maintenance mode" and then stayed in it basically indefinitely. (It's) bad for team morale, you lose the ability to prioritize your work, and you always feel like you're on a treadmill.
>
> I also think that a lot of agile practices have "fallback modes" that teams can easily get trapped in—the fallback mode is less work than the full agile practice but also way less effective. I think that event driven is the fallback mode of agile planning.

Very occasionally, organizing a team as a kind of human event-handling system is the correct thing to do. But it should not be the default behavior. Instead, look for ways of decoupling these events, letting people poll for things they can do, rather than being forced.

Email, shared task lists, and Kanban boards are all ways of decoupling. When Andy and I were writing the second edition of *The Pragmatic Programmer*, we followed the same workflow we used 20 years previously: someone writes something and passes it over for review. The reviewer makes changes, then passes it back, and so on until no one has a change to make, at which point that writing goes into the book. (Where, of course, it is rewritten again.)

To organize this, we used a Kanban board on GitLab. Each chunk of text was represented by a card, and the column that the card was in represented the stage of the workflow. As we swapped content back and forth, we moved the card into a Review column and changed the assignee to the other person. That way we communicated asynchronously; when someone finished a chunk of work, they'd update the board and see immediately any new tasks.

| Idea 12 | **Find ways to interact asynchronously** |

Nothing's revolutionary about this; you might well be doing something similar with your coding tasks. But what else can you decouple using something like this? Do you need to wait for the result of a code review, or could you move on and then fix any internal problems after the review is complete? Obviously, it depends on what your typical review brings up. Might be worth exploring, though.

Do you have to couple people's time by making them attend meetings? Well, that's the next practice.

Try this

Keep a list of things that cause you to wait for other people during your working day. For each item, note the rough time you lost.

After a week or so, group these items into high-level categories, things such as *waiting for a meeting to start* or *waiting for a code review* or *need someone else's code to finish* or *waiting for a technical question to be answered*.

For each of these higher-level categories, spend some time thinking about how the wait could be eliminated or how the effect of the wait can be mitigated. Chat with others on your team to see if they're willing to experiment. If so, institute some changes and carry on collecting entries on your list. At the end of a month or two, total up the time you spent waiting, both before the experiment and after. Adjust as needed.

Meetings, Bloody Meetings

At the risk of channeling Donald Rumsfeld, for any particular person there are:

1. Things they know that they know.
2. Things they know that they don't know.
3. Things they don't know that they don't know.

The overall hope when running a meeting is that people in the first group will help enlighten those in groups two and three, and along the way, everyone will learn something.

The reality, though, is that meetings are often about those in groups one and three arguing about their personal realities, and those in group two catching up on their social media.

Sometimes a meeting is an appropriate tool. Most of the time, though, the meetings we hold are at best a waste of time and at worst a source of misinformation, confusion, and resentment.

Clearly, there are many levels of meeting: two people discussing an idea might be one end of the spectrum, while an all-hands meeting is at the other. I have nothing at all against two or three people meeting to discuss something (as long as they are aware of the Practice 6, Decorum: If You Have to Have a Meeting, on page 31, guidelines). But I have a strong aversion to large meetings, and I really dislike the prevalence of all-hands meetings in the so-called agile world.

But Meetings Are "Agile"

Every "agile" method highlights the importance of communication within the team. Surely meetings are a great way to ensure that people are all on the same page. Meetings are the forum for leveling knowledge and sharing understanding, no?

I don't think so.

| Idea 13 | **Meetings are not "agile"** |

And maybe, secretly, the big-A agile folks don't really believe it either given the recent trend to relabel meetings as "ceremonies." (Where did I put my ermine robe?)

Meetings Are Inefficient

Let's start this section by reminding ourselves that five minutes spent in a meeting with 12 participants represents at least a lost hour of overall productive time.

Why "at least"?

- Meetings often start late, and many meetings run over.

- Meetings often wait while a small group has a friendly, off-topic chat.

- Often there's a participant who just won't stop talking, often about things that may be only tangentially relevant.

- Many people won't have prepared, so the rest of the group will wait while they are brought up to speed.

- And my perennial favorite: the projector doesn't want to connect to the presenter's device.

On top of that, the format of most meetings does not encourage efficiency. Typically, one person talks, then people chime in with comments, and then those comments spark other comments, and so on. Then another person talks, and the comment cascade starts again. If this were an algorithm, it would be $O(n^2)$.

Idea 14	The negative impact of a meeting extends far beyond the meeting room

Meetings Are Unfair

It's all too easy for a meeting (particularly an online one) to be dominated by the most senior, most knowledgeable, most aggressive, or just least polite people present.

Even if you don't have a verbal bully in the room, shy or junior people often hold back unless the meeting leader explicitly involves them.

The result: the same people espouse the same viewpoints. Knowledge isn't shared; it's imposed.

Meetings Are Disruptive

Attending a meeting means stopping whatever you're doing at some appointed time. If you're in the middle of something, you have to stop. If you're in the flow, you have to stop. If you're in the middle of a conversation, you have to stop.

On its own, that can be disruptive. It's also time-wasting. If I know I have a meeting coming up, I'll typically not start something during the period of about 10 minutes before it starts. Sure, I'll try to fill in the time, but I won't be moving forward. Just as bad, after the meeting is over I have to come back and recapture the context of what I was doing—I probably waste 15 to 30 minutes coming back up to speed.

Meetings Are Expensive

Let's look at Scrum, not because it's worse than the others but because it is the most common, and its meetings are well documented. In a typical two-week sprint, a team will have the following all-hands meetings:

Meeting	Number	Hours/Per	Total Hours
Sprint Planning	1	4	4
Backlog Refinement	1	2	2
Daily Scrum	10	¼	2½
Sprint Review	1	2	2
Retrospective	1	3	3
TOTAL			13½

For one sprint, that's 13½ hours out of the total of 80 hours. If the overhead cost of a developer is $200/hour, and you have a team of 10 people, that's $27,000 every two weeks.

Is this time and money well spent?

Perhaps it is. But the only way to know is to measure, and the only way I can see to measure is to change what you do and see what the impact is.

So that's what this section is: a series of things that other teams have successfully adopted to overcome the problems with meetings. Let's start by establishing just why we have meetings.

(Oh, and if you were wondering about the title of this practice, have a look at this marvelous John Cleese training video.[1])

---

1.   https://vimeo.com/709207228

Idea 15   Meetings are inefficient, unfair, disruptive, and expensive

Why Meet at All?

I asked people *why* they had so many meetings. Ignoring the "because that's what we do" answers, here's what I heard:

- The daily standup gives people a chance to say what they've done, what they plan to do, and what problems they have. The intent is to help the team understand the overall context and perhaps to give individuals the chance to offer advice on problems someone else is facing.

- Design sessions help to thrash out architecture, design, and implementation issues. Alternatives are discussed, new ideas are injected, and more junior team members learn about new languages, frameworks, and patterns.

- Planning meetings give the team context, helping them understand what work is to be done and what the priorities are. It also gives folks a sense of ownership of the schedule.

- The review meetings are an opportunity for the team to celebrate successes and to understand, mitigate, and perhaps forgive, failures.

- All-hands meetings are also felt to be team-building events, where people get to know each other better and possibly trust each other more.

Are there other, more efficient ways, of getting the same benefits?

Developer Without Portfolio

Many of the successful teams I met with had created a new role. Some called it *project lead*, but to my mind that title has other baggage. Some called it *architect*, but again there's baggage. So I'm going to use *developer without portfolio*, or DWP.

The DWP's sole responsibility is to keep the team running smoothly and effectively. If the team is an engine, the DWP is the oil.

Idea 16	**Developer without portfolio reduces team friction**

To do this, the DWP talks with people. Not by having weekly meetings or daily chats, but by actually engaging. I spoke with a team where the DWP spent a lot of their time pair programming with random team members. On another team, the DWP would carry their laptop into different areas and set up shop, listening in to what was happening and chatting where appropriate. There's no rule here: it's up to the personality of the individual. Whatever mode they choose, though, the outcome should be the same: they should know what everyone is doing, their pain points and misunderstandings, their successes and their frustrations.

Knowing all this, the DWP then works to remove impediments.

Replacing the Daily Standup Meeting

The DWP is constantly building a picture of the team's overall situation, sharing and updating it as they circulate through the team. They make a point of asking people what they're planning to do and what problems they're facing.

When people describe their plans, the DWP can slot that into the overall project context. They may discover that the planned work might not be needed, or they may notice that another team member had written some code that might help.

If the developer is having problems, the DWP will come up with ways to help. For small issues, this might be as simple as directly explaining something to the developer. For bigger things, though, the DWP's job is to put the developer in touch with other team members who can help.

During this process, the DWP is also monitoring progress.

Streamlining the Review Meetings

The DWP will already have a good picture of how a development has gone. They will have seen issues and misunderstandings arise, notice tasks where estimates were off, and seen people succeed or struggle.

So rather that the typical "so let's go 'round the room" review, the DWP can circulate their observations ahead of the meeting, allowing the team to focus on resolutions.

Streamlining Design Meetings

The DWP is explicitly *not* the team architect and should have no special authority when it comes to design decisions. However, of all the team's members, the DWP probably has the best overall picture of what is needed. Combined with the DWP's experience, this puts them into a good position to make suggestions and outline alternatives when it comes to design.

At the same time, design is often best when done collaboratively, which probably calls for meetings. My strong suggestion: limit the attendance to three or four people and try to follow the decorum guidelines at the end of the chapter.

You Expect Us to Add an Extra Team Member Who Isn't Coding?

I don't expect it, but I hope you'll try it.

If you need help justifying it, add up the developer hours currently spent in meetings. For the team of 10 developers we talked about in Meetings Are Expensive, on page 26, that figure comes to about 135 hours per two-week sprint. If you eliminate those meetings by adding a DWP, that's equivalent to adding over one and a half extra developers to the team. Even if you only halve the time spent in meetings, you've freed up the equivalent of 80 percent of one developer's time. The other advantages of a DWP will easily make up the extra 20 percent.

Some Meetings Are Unavoidable

All-hands meetings are definitely appropriate when they address things that genuinely impact the entire team, such as project inception, large project windup, and company announcements. If you have any control over these, try to follow the meeting decorum guidelines that follow.

Other meetings will also be necessary: design sessions, management reporting, subteam coordination, and so on. Keep these small—you can always bring people in if needed. Follow meeting decorum.

Try this		

Discuss the concept of a developer without portfolio, first with your team and later with managers. If everyone's on board, run an experiment.

Decide what metrics are important, and make sure you have them available for the three months before the experiment.

During this time, cast around for someone who can take on the DWP role. They should be fairly experienced, enjoy chatting with people, and be capable of putting aside their own opinions.

Then take a couple of months migrating to the new way of working and start collecting the metrics again. Six months later, compare metrics and decide whether to continue.

All I ask is that, alongside all the regular performance metrics, you also include some measures of developer sentiment.

Decorum: If You Have to Have a Meeting

The meetings I dread are announced when someone says, "Let's get a group together and talk about X." It's pretty much guaranteed that such an ad hoc meeting will be unstructured, unproductive, and potentially unpleasant.

I'm not totally against meetings. But if a meeting has to happen, then we should do our best to make it pleasant and productive. And that means that someone has to take responsibility for organizing it and running it.

Running a meeting considerately and effectively involves the following:

- Having a clear objective
- Verifying that a meeting is needed
- Preparation
- Selecting attendees
- Scheduling
- Direction
- Wrap-up and follow-up

This is all basic stuff, but it's normally ignored or done half-heartedly. This is one of those times where simplicity (and efficiency) comes from following the rules.

Idea 17	**The only good meeting is a well-prepared one**

Clear Objective

The objective is the answer to the question, "Why do I want to have this meeting, anyway?"

As with every agile action, this objective must be measurable: did the meeting achieve what it was meant to?

This means that the objective you set must be bounded and measurable. Here are some good objectives:

- Plan the handover of the sales module from the red team to the blue team.

  This can be verified at the end of the meeting by getting the participants to run through the plan.

- Agree support staff vacation schedule over the holiday season.

  The verification is that you walk away with a calendar showing when every support person is available and that there are no gaps in coverage.

- Ensure operations have what they need to migrate the database schema.

  Before the meeting ends, you'll want to run through the migration plan and have everyone agree that it seems solid.

Here are some bad meeting objectives:

- Discuss the deployment of the next release.

  Nothing's wrong with discussion, but it's not an objective. What is the *result* of all the talking? How can you measure it? The objective needs to be clear and specific.

- Improve project estimates.

  Perhaps a worthy goal, but there's no measurable outcome from the meeting itself. Perhaps the meeting objective is "Identify one thing that a previous estimate got wrong and come up with a way to prevent a recurrence."

Is a Meeting Needed?

All too often, meetings are called because it's easier than doing the work. So be honest with yourself—could you save overall effort if you invested some time yourself and spared other team members.

The previous example of agreeing vacation dates is a good example. Why do you need everyone in a room when you all have access to a shared calendar? Sure, there may be conflicts, and that's where you'll need to invest some energy. But in terms of overall effort, it's a clear win.

Be creative when it comes to avoiding unnecessary meetings.

Flip This Meeting

When I went to school, we learned lessons during school time and then tested our knowledge with homework.

Some schools now turn that on its head. In the *flipped-classroom* model, students learn the material on their own, before the class, using materials prepared by the teacher. They then attend the lesson, where the class works on activities that solidify that understanding, while the teacher offers guidance and help.

Too often we run meetings like traditional school rooms. You attend to hear a lecture and then get assigned work to do back at your desk.

There's never an excuse to give a long lecture in a meeting; you brought your colleagues together to solve a problem, not listen to the issues.

So flip your meetings. Before you even announce the meeting, prepare materials that you'll give to attendees before they arrive. These materials will cover any background they need, so everyone can hit the ground running once they're together.

Idea 18	Flip meetings: share before, examine during

Depending on your style, you may choose to create an agenda. My recommendation here is to try meetings both with and without one and see which goes better.

I find a secret benefit of doing this. Often, as I prepare the materials, I find myself realizing that I misunderstood the problem. The need for the meeting evaporates. Everyone wins.

Selecting Attendees

Parsimony is the name of the game here. Once you've prepared your briefing materials, choose the key people who need to be there, the people who are needed to reach an outcome. Send them a summary and ask if they feel they should attend. If they agree, perhaps ask if your attendee list is missing anyone.

The smaller the group, the better the discussion and the faster the meeting.

Scheduling

A bunch of folklore surrounds the best time to schedule meetings. Avoid the slot after lunch; people are sleepy. Avoid the end of the day; people want to go home. Avoid Monday morning; people are busy catching up. And so on.

I don't think there's one good time to have meetings. But you can be considerate of other people. Remember that a meeting basically interrupts whatever all the attendees were doing. Maybe try to schedule meetings that start at natural breaks—first thing in the morning, perhaps.

And if you have people in many time zones, be considerate. If the working days just don't overlap, alternate who has to get up early.

Or, better yet, don't have a meeting.

Direct

If you've arranged a meeting, then it's your responsibility to make sure that everyone gets value from it, and that means that you're going to have to guide things along.

Start on time, and don't recapitulate for latecomers.

Make sure everyone understands what the measurable outcomes of the meeting are. If you have an agenda, follow it.

Make sure everyone is heard. This may involve gently shutting down folks who like to talk. Sometimes two people will get into a debate. That's fine for one or two exchanges, but after that step in with "So Jan thinks X and Pat thinks Y. Anyone have any thoughts?"

I hate meetings where multiple discussions happen at once. A classic way to avoid having to police this is to bring some kind of token to meetings and make a rule that people can only speak when they're in possession of that token; yes, it's a real-world semaphore. If nothing else, a whole lot of quiet satisfaction is to be derived from telling a VP that they can't speak yet because they don't have Mr. Squeaky.

One of the roles of the person who called the meeting is to moderate the discussion, preventing these private discussions, while also encouraging the quiet participants to say their piece. In the end, if the moderator models, and if necessary enforces, respect, people will learn.

One of the trickiest parts of running a meeting is pacing. You want to make sure you achieve the meeting's objective at or before the end time. I've found it useful to jot down some milestones and times before the meeting starts. Not only does this help get the timing right, it also gives you a kind of road map to steer the conversation.

A rookie mistake is to reach the end of a meeting and then simply disperse. Always allow a couple of minutes for a wrap-up.

Wrap Up. Follow Up

Remember, your meeting needs a measurable objective. Simply having everyone agree is not enough. Run through the outcome, stating each point of agreement, and make sure you or the meeting scribe writes it down.

Thank everyone for their time. Send them on their way at or before the scheduled end time.

After the meeting, take some time to compare the actual outcome to the target. Did your meeting achieve what you wanted? Either way, jot a quick note to every attendee summarizing what was done and how it will affect things going forward.

Exploratory Meetings

In one kind of meeting these suggestions don't apply. An example is the initial get-together of the 17 middle-aged white guys (sad, but true) where we created the Manifesto for Agile Software Development. Going in, the only thing we knew was that we wanted to compare ideas about software development practices and possibly find some common ground. We had no plan and no agenda.

Idea 19	**Exploratory meetings have different rules**

We started by removing the table and organizing the chairs in an oval. After we introduced ourselves, someone passed around a bunch of index cards. We each wrote down things we felt were important to discuss, one thing per card. We then had a lot of fun seeing how accurately we could frisbee the cards into a pile.

We took a break while someone organized the cards into topics, and then we held a dot vote to set the order we'd address them. That order held for maybe 90 minutes, but by then we'd covered enough ground that we came up with an initial set of "we value X over Y" statements over lunch.

Exploratory meetings are very different from decision-making meetings, and they're a lot harder to get right. I know some people will only hold exploratory meetings if they hire an external moderator to run them. I've only experienced one such meeting; I have to say it went very well.

Dot Votes

A dot vote allows a group of people to collectively choose among options. The distinguishing feature is that every person gets more than one vote. They can use all their votes on a single item or spread votes between many items. In the end, the number of votes an item has garnered determines its rank.

For a list of 10 items, you'd normally give everyone three or maybe four votes. Sometimes you may want to give stakeholders an extra vote or two to increase their influence on the outcome.

It's called a dot vote because traditionally you wrote the items on a whiteboard and then people went up and put colored dots against their choices.

Try this

If your role is typically that of a meeting attendee, and not an organizer, you're in a great position to learn what works and what doesn't. Maybe take notes (discretely); one day you'll be running your own meetings. These notes will help you hit the ground running.

Model decorum

This one can be difficult. When you attend meetings, try to act the way you wish everyone else would act. See if you can get some like-minded colleagues to go along.

Run simple

If part of your role is to run meetings, start to introduce these practices. Explain to attendees what you're doing and why you're doing it. Ask for their help. And remember to get feedback.

And remember:

| Idea 20 | **Play nicely** |

Spread Your Skills

In learning, you will teach, and in teaching, you will learn.
> *Phil Collins, Son of Man*

I learned a surprising lesson back in the mid 2000s. A conference I was attending had organized a room where programmers who were just starting out could pair with more experienced attendees. I went in for a couple of hours; at that point I was most likely one of the western world's most experienced Ruby programmers. It would be good to bestow nuggets of wisdom on some lucky students.

In those couple of hours I probably learned more about programming than I had in the previous two years. After half-a-dozen years of programming Ruby, I'd settled into a style that worked for me; I attacked problems in the same way, and I used the same idioms while coding. And the students I sat with undermined all of that with just one word.

Why?

Why are you using each to write for-loops? Why do array indices start at zero? Why do you always call your index variables i? Why, why, why?

It was like coding with precocious three-year-olds. But every single question made me stop and think. I'm sure they were surprised when they asked a seemingly basic question and I went quiet for 30 seconds, trying to come up with a reason that could survive inspection.

It wasn't just their questions. I also had to reach way inside to come up with ways to explain concepts to newcomers to the craft. How could I describe a Hash or a File object in ways that both made sense and that were useful abstractions?

I came away from these sessions both pumped up and exhausted. And I'd learned something that most of you already know. To quote Phil Collins, "In teaching you will learn."

Sharing Skills Amplifies Skills

If you share your candy bar, you end up eating less of it. But if you share your skills, both your student and you end up with more. It's a *positive-sum game.*[2]

And that's the selfish reason to share—it makes you a better developer.

Idea 21	Teach to learn

But obviously, there's another side to the equation: the person you share with is also gaining from your experience and wisdom. They get stronger, and your team gets stronger.

Equality Is Not the Goal

If ever there was a team whose every member was equally proficient in every skill, it would be horribly inefficient. Specialization allows the team to benefit from the variety of knowledge and experience of its members. This variety also increases the team's resilience.

Marmorkrebs crayfish, cheetahs, and the Channel Island fox are examples of species with very little genetic diversity between members. This makes them fragile. If an environmental change or disease affects one, it affects them all.

It's the same with homogeneous teams. If they are all experts in Java and Oracle, and the world moves to Postgres and JavaScript, the team as a whole is suddenly obsolete.

Let's try to visualize this. We'll assume a team has five members. Each has varying experience, rated 0 to 5, in three databases (Postgres, Oracle, and MySQL), three languages (Java, JavaScript, and Rust), and three environments (back end, front end, and SPAs). We'll capture the nine experience numbers from each team member and represent them in a grid: databases in the first column, languages in the second, and environments in the third. Around each number we'll draw a circle whose area is proportional to that number. Here's what this might look like for a team where each member has different skills:

---

2.   https://www.britannica.com/topic/positive-sum-game

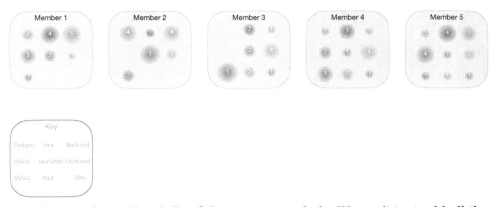

Now let's work out the skills of the team as a whole. We can't just add all the corresponding numbers: if member 1 has level 4 experience in Oracle and member 2 is level 3, then the chances are good that a lot of what they know overlaps. So, for no other reason that it seemed to be a good idea, I calculated a total experience for each topic by sorting the individual values and giving the first a weighting of 1, the next 1/2, then 1/4, 1/8, and 1/16.

After cranking the adding machine handle, we get the following:

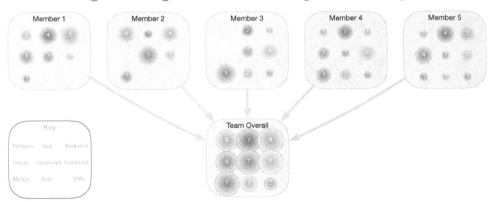

That looks like a pretty healthy coverage.

Now let's look at the homogeneous team, with all their skills in Oracle, Java, and back-end development.

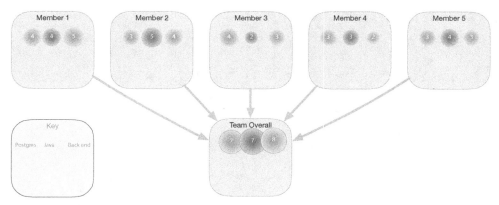

The overall team skills are looking a little sparse. And compare the top row in the team skills box to the top row for the team with mixed skills. Even though people in the first team are weaker individually in Oracle, Java, and back-end development, the overall team skills for those three areas are not much lower: when you add skills, there's a lot of overlap.

| Idea 22 | All experience is useful. Diverse experience teaches more |

When you're building teams, by all means look for the skills you directly need, but not to the exclusion of the occasional wild card. If you're choosing a team to join, you'll learn more if their main focus is slightly outside your personal comfort zone. Diversity is resiliency, both among members of an animal species and between developers on a team.

Become a teacher and a student

Get used to the quiet rhythm of helping people—sharing your experience without being intrusive.

If you find yourself wanting to correct someone, stop and think before acting. What led them to make the mistake? Rather than fixing the problem, could you explore the cause of the problem with them and let them work out the fix for themselves?

And if someone finds a problem in your work, try not to react defensively. Instead, think about what they said. If you understand the issues, thank them. If you don't, ask them to dig a little deeper so you can learn the underlying cause of your mistake.

What good teachers do

Most of us probably have a teacher or two who changed our lives for the better; mine was Mr. Knight, code name Albert, who taught maths (yes, it had an "s"; it was in England) and was also my homeroom teacher for three years.

These key teachers have a way of engaging that makes you feel part of the learning process; you're engaged because they are. It's partly a question of personality but also has aspects that can be learned.

Good teachers feel they have a mission, and they like to talk about it. I find it encouraging (and humbling) to read their stories. Here's a short list of things I read while writing this:

- https://www.nu.edu/blog/qualities-of-a-good-teacher/
- https://www.teachersoftomorrow.org/blog/insights/good-teacher-qualities/
- https://www.wgu.edu/blog/top-qualities-skills-good-teacher2001.html

You'll need to adjust these, as they're aimed at a classroom environment, but then again, good teachers are adaptable.

Thank a teacher today

Is that special teacher in your life still around? Why not get in touch and thank them. See what they're up to. And rehear all the horror stories of when you were in school.

If you're a parent, maybe your children have a teacher that changed them. Perhaps an informal "thank you" at the end of the school year might be in order.

Practice 8

Let the Information Go Free

Communication involves more than the mechanics of person A communicating with person B. The successful teams I spoke with all insisted that information needs to be freely available. Some talked about making it easy to ask, and others talked about creating the kind of environment where information is ambient and team members absorb much of it without even realizing it. Whatever you do, communication needs active management so that information can flow.

Let's look at some ideas.

Eliminate Information Silos

It's only natural. If you work as part of a small team on a particular corner of a project, you become invested in that team. Your team probably has its own jargon specific to the concepts in your code, and you use shorthand to talk about functionality and design. As time goes on, this makes it increasingly difficult to talk about your work with other developers; before you can chat about the cool stuff, you'd have to fill them in on a lot of background.

As a result, we tend not to bother. Information and knowledge become localized to each small team, forming *information silos*.

> **Idea 23** **Knowledge hoarded is knowledge that's rotting**

But knowledge shared is knowledge multiplied. When you share knowledge with others, you're not just giving it away. You're giving them new ideas that augment their existing knowledge. And those new ideas don't just sit there; they interact with all the existing ideas, synthesizing brand-new intuitions. The sum of two pieces of knowledge is more than two pieces of knowledge.

Spread Yourself Around

Here are some ways that teams that value knowledge transfer make it work.

First, they make it explicit that everyone on the team has something to teach and something to learn. They explain the big difference between teaching and just telling someone what to do; teaching is a process of discovery, where the teacher acts as a guide and a coach and not as an all-knowing oracle. The teams are encouraged to ask questions and discuss issues. And they're also told that sometimes the answers have to be discovered through experimentation: the old orient-step-learn loop.

Given that background and given that we've discovered that mixing things up makes them stronger, these successful teams all use one or more of the following to help disperse skills.

Pair programming

Rotate pairs fairly frequently, and make sure that everyone gets to pair with everyone else over time.

Developer without portfolio

One of the DWP responsibilities is to put people with a question in touch with people with an answer. Sometimes, the DWP doesn't even wait for the explicit question: if they spot someone struggling, they'll ask someone to wander over and help.

Brown-bag lunches

Folks get together over lunch and discuss things that interest them. Sometimes these are book clubs, where they discuss a chapter a week. Sometimes they ask members to take turns talking about something cool they found.

Developer shuffle

Every few months the department plays musical chairs, moving one developer from each team to another. This obviously spreads knowledge. But it also gives individuals a chance to experience different problem domains—sometimes people find their passion this way. It also has a couple of interesting side effects. First, projects that have been stuck for a while often get a fresh perspective. Second, when a team inducts a new member, they get to see their code through fresh eyes, often triggering a round of cleanup and refactoring.

Code reviews

Have people from outside the team perform code reviews.

Mob rule

Merge several teams for a day and have them mob code a solution to one of the more general problems they need to solve: improving logging, speeding up the build, updating libraries, or whatever.

Skill mix

Construct teams containing people with complementary skills. This way, the team can't help but share knowledge.

Experience diversity

Construct teams containing people with different levels of experience. Junior developers will benefit from the experience of the old hands. At the same time, the questions the juniors ask will often trigger the old hands to think about things they've taken for granted. I personally love being in both roles at different times. I'm always learning new things.

One thing to avoid: the difference in experience should not be so great that the two developers just can't communicate. Very experienced developers work largely by intuition and not using the more prescriptive patterns used by beginners. Often, the only answer a wizard can give is "it's obvious," which helps no one.

Formal training

If a department changes one of their technology platforms, they often set aside a few days to help people get up to speed. I've heard mixed reports on these sessions; in some cases they go really well, and in others people come away not much wiser. I suspect the difference comes down to the preparation and the enthusiasm of the teacher.

Friday playtime

A couple of teams I contacted set aside a half day a week for non-project work. They encourage people to pair, where one person in the pair instigates the project and the second person wants to learn about it. These projects could involve working on tools, learning a new language, experimenting with ESP32s—whatever sounds interesting.

| Idea 24 | **Knowledge shared is knowledge multiplied** |

The "Friday playtime" example illustrates an important point. Skills transfer (and learning in general) does not have to be focused on work-related technologies to be beneficial. Software is one of those industries where skills transfer easily between specialties.

However...

In his review of a draft of this book, Noel Rappin made a great point:

> In larger organizations you really, really need management buy-in to make a lot of these things work because they all work against manager incentives, which are normally focused on the short term.

> If management doesn't agree, everybody will continually beg off doing these kinds of things because they are too busy.

And, of course, persuading higher-management needs communication skills...

Pick an activity

Choose something from the preceding list that your team is not currently doing and try to make it happen. This may involve selling it to other team members and possibly some negotiating with management. Tell them Dave sent you.

Part II

Simplify Your Environment

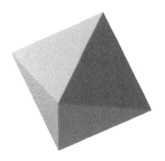

## CHAPTER 4

Automate All the Things

I have an arachnoid cyst in my brain. It's a 6 cm void in my left temporal lobe where hearing discrimination and part of my memory is supposed to be. As a result, I can't make out what people are saying when I'm in a crowd, and I can't remember the stuff I want to remember (yet I can recall the license plate number of my first car).

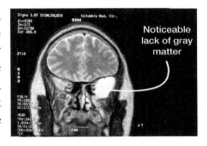

Noticeable lack of gray matter

I compensate for the first with a combination of lip-reading and laughing when other people laugh. For the second, I try to offload stuff to external devices: my daybook,[1] lists, calendars, notes on the fridge, and so on.

When it comes to software, one of my most important techniques for dealing with my lack of brain mass is automation. The more I automate, the less I have to remember. If I can deploy by pushing a button or typing a command, I don't have to scrabble around to find a checklist. (It also means I won't miss step 17.)

If I automatically run tests when I save a source file, I don't have to have some part of my brain looping around asking me "did you run the tests?" If I automate my environment setup, then I won't waste time tracking down why some library version is wrong.

I don't think I'm alone in this. The good developers I watch all create automations to reduce the cognitive load of creating software. The less we have to remember, the less stress we have. We're happier, and we create better software.

So here are some of the areas I automate. As always, your focus will be different from mine, and the tools you choose are up to you.

---

1. https://articles.pragdave.me/p/why-you-need-a-daybook

Practice 9

Make Your Desktop Work for You

I spend far too long every day looking at a rectangle of dark plastic covered by what my wife calls "teeny-tiny writing." This is my window into the abstraction we call software development. I use it to create and maintain code, to run programs, to do research, and to watch cat videos.

It makes sense to do as much as I can to tailor this environment to both my needs and the projects I'm working on. That involves two main things: trying every single damn color scheme I can find and automating as much as I can.

Workspaces

Like everyone, I do many different things during the day. Sometimes I'm writing books, other times updating the PragProg tool chain, handling email, or looking at social media and the web.

Like many people, I don't have much discipline. I could be coding away and then the email window updates, so of course I have to stop what I'm doing to see what just came in. I know I shouldn't, but...

Idea 25	**Organize your desktop as you organize your time**

My solution to this is to set up workspaces. These are complete desktops, each with their own windows and apps, which I can switch between on my display. It's like having multiple displays but arranged so you can only look at one at a time.

One desktop has my email and a browser window (because answering an email often involves accessing some web content).

If I'm writing, I'll have a workspace containing my editor, my book builder, and a PDF previewer. (Here's what it looks like, although my fonts are smaller IRL.)

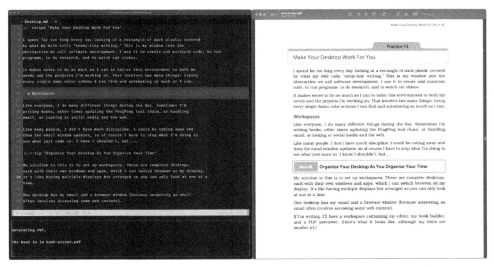

I'll then have a workspace for each project I'm working on.

The joy of this setup is that I can switch away from what I'm doing and then later switch back to find it exactly as I left it. I don't get distracted, and I'm less likely to end up with a screen containing 168 overlapping windows.

This simplifies my life tremendously while making me feel more productive.

What Do I Use?

I do most of my work on OS X, wandering over to my Linux box every now and then. On the Mac, I used to use the built-in Spaces feature of OS X. That could be painful at times, and the lack of full keyboard control was annoying. Now I use a tiling window manager and love it.

Windows are laid out in horizontal and vertical stacks, and they don't overlap. Initially I thought this was going to be a showstopper for me, but I've actually come to appreciate how much cleaner it feels to use. And, with full keyboard control, I can fling windows between workspaces without reaching for a mouse.

Watch yourself working

You might not think that it's worth the hassle of learning a window manager's key-bindings; it might not be.

But do me a favor—watch how you currently manage your screen real estate while you work. Are you doing a lot of alt-tabbing to find the window you want? Do you periodically have to go on a window purge? Do you have to use a mouse to navigate?

If so, it might be worth experimenting for a week with a tool that can manage your windows and workspaces.

Try out workspaces

If you're not currently using workspaces, have a look around for tools that let you try it in your environment.

Give it a go for a week. It will take you a couple of days to get the configuration set the way you want. After that, try to develop the habit to partition your work, and see if the experience works for you.

Try out window managers

Even if you're not sold on the idea of workspaces, play around with tiling window managers—there are many to choose from. If you've never used one, you might be frustrated at first: you're used to having 207 windows open, and that just doesn't work when they're all visible. Perhaps that's the point. Do you really need all 207 windows at the same time?

Practice 10

Make Your Terminal Work for You

First things first. I live in the terminal, but many of you do not. I try hard not to tell you what to do, but I'm about to make an exception.

| Idea 26 | **Effective developers know their way around the terminal** |

I use the terminal because it gives me superpowers. Everything that I can do with the computer is only a few keystrokes away. Even better, I can combine commands in lots of different ways: I can run them sequentially, send the output of one to the input of another, or use one command as the argument to another. I'm working with plain text, and over the years people have developed large numbers of utilities that will process that text in any way imaginable.

When you do all of your work through GUI applications, you're limited to the capabilities built into those apps. This is sometimes referred to as What You See Is All You Get (as opposed to What You See Is What You Get, or WYSI-WYG). For specialist tasks, such as image editing, this is acceptable. But productive programmers have unpredictable needs. Knowing your shell simplifies how you work when you reach the limits of your GUI applications.

When you use your terminal, you have access to the entire underlying operating system; I can write scripts and combine applications to achieve pretty much anything I might need.

Here are some terminal commands that illustrate the kind of things I do on a daily basis:

```
# rename all the .ts files in src/ to have a .bak extension
$ mv src/*.{ts,bak}
```

```
# How many words do I have in my book (ish)
$ wc -w **md
```

```
# Build the book from source whenever a file changes
$ ls **md | entr ./rake clean screen
```

```
# Where have I used the English spelling of color (in any case)?
$ rg -i colour
```

```
# Fetch a JSON document containing information on the Pokemon Mewtwo,
# and print a list of its moves
$ curl -s 'https://pokeapi.co/api/v2/pokemon/mewtwo' | jq -r '.moves[] | .move.name'
```

OK, so I don't fetch Pokemon information on a daily basis (or ever, really). But I do use a similar-looking command to try out JSON APIs and sometimes to produce ad hoc reports from my own systems.

Shell? Terminal? What's the Difference?

Back when dinosaurs roamed the earth, we connected to central computers over phone lines. To do this, we used a terminal: a device with a keyboard and a means of displaying characters (initially a paper roll and a typewriter mechanism and later a CRT display).

Once we connected, we had to have a way of interacting with the machine and telling it what to do. Typically it worked this way: the computer would get notified that an incoming line was ringing. It would answer the call and establish a data connection. It would then spawn a program, attaching its input and output to that connection. Everything the user typed would be sent to this program, and everything the program output would be sent back to the terminal.

This program had various names, but people eventually settled on *shell* or *command shell.*

Today's computers are structured differently but still use the same basic idea. Creating a new window establishes a connection to an application. One kind of application is a *terminal emulator,* which pretends to be a very sophisticated physical terminal. Rather than calling our computer using the phone, it establishes a connection by opening a device called a *pseudo-teletype,* or pty. When that connection is made, the operating system gets a notification exactly as if the phone had rung, and it accepts the call and starts a shell.

So two components cooperate to let you type commands at your computer: the terminal and the shell. And, lucky you, there are a wide variety of both to choose from—you can totally own how it looks and works.

Getting Started

The *terminal* is just an application like any other. Most computers ship with a terminal app: on OS X it's called *Terminal,* on Linux it might be *xterm,* and on Windows the default is called *cmd.*

These terminals work well, and they're probably the ones you should use when getting started. Eventually you'll probably want to install more sophisticated terminal apps, which I'll talk about in a bit.

Where I have the most fun is the shell.

All shells have the same basic functions. They prompt you to enter commands and then run those commands. They let you redirect where those commands get their input from and where their output goes. They keep a history of the commands you enter, and they let you recall and edit previous commands.

The feature that simplifies my life the most is called *completion*. As I'm typing, I can hit the ↹ key, and the shell will try to complete what I'm typing with something that makes sense given the context: a command name, a file name, or even options specific to the command I'm trying to run.

All shells also support scripting, where you can automate a sequence of commands using their own built-in language.

Extras That I Look For: The Terminal

When evaluating a terminal program, here's what I look for:

Speed
> Nowadays the baseline for terminal emulators is to use GPU rendering, so output should scroll by very quickly. (I just tried it on my Mac Mini, and my terminal scrolled through a 16,000-line file in 45 ms.)

Scrollback
> The terminal should be able to retain at least the last 2,000 lines of output, and ideally more. Modern log files are incredibly verbose, and you sometimes need that kind of buffer to scroll back to the actual error.

Themes
> It sounds trivial, but I've worked hard to select a theme that doesn't leave me with sore eyes or a headache at the end of a day.

Key mapping
> It's very convenient to be able to have both my terminal and my editor use the same keys for things such as window switching.

Multiple panes/windows
> For me, this is a must; a short explanation is next.

| Idea 27 | The terminal does the presentation |

Multiple Panes

I want a terminal that lets me split my window into multiple panes and run a separate shell in each pane. I need the layout of these panes to be configurable, and I want to be able to control the font sizes in each pane independently (because I often leave logs scrolling in a separate window, tucked out of the way but still visible).

Some people do this using a terminal multiplexer—tmux is the poster child for this. I don't need all the fancy session management stuff that tmux provides, so running it means yet one more set of key sequences to learn.

Instead, I use a terminal that lets me create and layout panes directly, using just the keyboard. I then set up key mappings so that the same sequences move me between terminal windows and editor buffers.

Extras I Look For: The Shell

I have fallen in love with contextual command completion. Every shell lets you type edit intro `→|`; it will look for a file whose name starts "intro" and suggest the available names for you to pick.

Most shells will also provide a similar thing at the command level. Type ed `→|` and it will suggest commands starting with "ed".

Contextual completion takes this a step further and remembers the commands you entered and the directory you were in when you entered them. The shell will then preferentially suggest completions that match the current directory.

It sounds trivial, but in practice it makes a major difference, particularly if you set up different workspaces for different tasks. When you switch to a new workspace, your shell makes suggestions that are local to the directory of that workspace, increasing the feeling of each space being distinct.

I also look for a decent scripting language. Many shells are POSIX compliant, and their scripting languages look similar. The languages are powerful but also incredibly arcane. I'm not a full-time writer of shell scripts, so I'd like to be able to code at a more humane level.

| Idea 28 | **The shell gives you power** |

My Current Daily Drivers

On my Macs I use Kitty as my terminal and Fish as my shell. You should choose for yourself—test out different options until you find ones that work for you.

Explore, experiment, play, optimize, and customize

- Do you currently use your terminal app? If not, start it up and play with it. See how to change your current directory, list the files in it, display a text file on the terminal, and search for all occurrences of some word in all the files in the directory.

- If you don't use your terminal, the next time you need to update your local files from your version control repository, work out how to do it from the terminal. After that, see if you can build and run the project.

- Customize your terminal: set up the keyboard shortcuts and the color scheme that suits you. Customize your shell—many a happy hour can be spent getting your prompt just right. Have a look online for some of the totally over-the-top prompts people have created.

- How long can you go without using a mouse? It took some time, but now when coding I can go all day. How about you?

- If you're an experienced terminal and shell user, keep a list of things that frustrate you about the experience. Once in a while, scan for new or updated terminals and shells that might alleviate the problem.

Practice 11

Automate Everything Else

When I were a lad, we'd build our systems by running compilers and then linking the object files into an executable image. We'd then manually copy that image up to some other computer, edit a few configuration files, restart the target machine, and hope.

Not surprisingly, building and deploying was always a scary business, and we frequently crashed systems, deployed the wrong app versions, and generally messed up production systems in every imaginable way.

Today, we have plenty of tools that handle the building, deploying, and updating of our systems. They ensure consistency and repeatability and often let you roll releases back in case of problems.

These tools are perhaps the biggest factor contributing to the reliability of our running applications.

Idea 29	**Automation == Reliability**

From a developer's viewpoint, they are also massively simpler and less stressful than the manual alternatives.

All of which makes it insane that there are still teams who don't use them.

Automate First, Code Second

I use a trivial trick to make sure that I don't leave automating my projects to chance.

When I start a new project, the first hour or so is always spent getting the environment set up. Sometimes I'm using a framework that generates much of it for me; other times I start with a bare directory and create the structure for myself.

Whichever path I take, I have a rule. Before I write a line of application code, I have to be able to do these things:

1. Delete my local copy of the project files and reconstitute them from a version control system somewhere.

2. Install all my project dependencies with a single command.

3. Use a single command to build my project from source (although that source will probably just be a "Hello, World!" program).

4. Run my tests, either automatically as part of the build or with a single command.

5. Deploy my project to its target environment.

That sounds like a lot of work. In practice, if you do this regularly, you'll quickly build up a set of template projects that have all of these features in place, requiring just a little customization.

But why do this before I have any code? Because I've learned (the hard way) that if I don't, then I'll keep pushing it off; getting the next feature working always seems like a higher priority than administrative housekeeping.

In the past, I was normally pretty good about steps one through four. Deployment, though, tended to be an afterthought. And as a result, it was always a nightmare.

If instead you deploy your application on day zero, it should be simple. You have no additional environment to set up, no database to initialize, no mailer to configure, no message queue to start—you're just running "Hello, World!" on some other machine. Get that working, and then start adding to your app. As you do, keep deploying it. At some point you'll need a database, so on the next deploy you'll need to work out how to provision it and initialize the schema.

But doing that as you go along is so much simpler than trying to get the entire finished application configured and running at the same time. If you leave deployment to the end, then you'll have to get *every* moving part working perfectly before you can test *anything*. You're never sure whether your application is failing because of a database issue, because there's a missing environment variable, or because the URL of the message queue has a typo.

Here's another big advantage to this approach. I tend to spin up a cheap server at my cloud provider, point a whimsical DNS name at it, and then deploy my app to it, often many times a day. This tells me that I'm able to do the deployment. But just as importantly, it means the people I'm writing the software for can play with the latest changes any time they want to. If I have a question, I can ask them to visit a particular place in the app and show them what I'm talking about.

Single Command Deployment Is Not Just Pushing the App

I'm sure you've come across something like this:

Deploy your Whizzo app with a single command! All you need is a one-time setup of your server, and then you're good to go.

To set up the server:

1. Provision a new Unix system.
2. Run apt get update then apt get install package1 package2 ... package39.
3. Create an application user and group.
4. Create a deploy directory and set ownership to that user.
5. Edit /etc/xxx....

   ...

   ...

46. Remove the temporary files created in step 35.
47. Edit the local file whizzo.yml to point to your new server.

Now, just type whizzo deploy. That single command will get your app up and running. Amazing, eh?

All fine and dandy if all you need to do is deploy new versions of the app. What happens if you need to deploy five new servers in an emergency?

Sometimes the answer to this is to use a managed application hosting environment, where all the setup steps have been done for you, and you just provide the application. Sometimes the answer is to deploy using containers or possibly use WASM. I personally like to use Ansible to handle both the server and the application setup and update.

Whatever mechanism you use, there's just one golden rule. Once you have a fresh target system powered on and provisioned with an SSH key, you should be able to configure the operating system, load your dependencies, get all the services running, deploy your application, configure it, migrate any data, and set it all running. And you should be able to do it with a single deployment command.

> **Idea 30** **Bare machine to running app with a single command**

Ideally, that command will be composed of a number of subcommands so that you can skip initial environment setup on an already set-up machine.

Don't Leave It to Chance

I always try to get this single-command deployment working on day 0. That means that as my application grows, and as it starts to use new resources, I can update the provisioning scripts alongside the application's code.

About once a week during development I'll reset my remote machine back to its bare state—an OS and an SSH key—and make sure I can still get the app running using the deployment command.

One day, at three in the morning and with all the sirens blaring, you'll be grateful you did.

Try it out

When you get a spare hour or two, create a "Hello, World!" app using the language and framework of your choice. Then create an automation that will deploy and run that app, starting with a fresh checkout and a newly minted target environment and ending up with your app deployed and running.

Make a change to the app and then update it on the target machine.

If you don't have time...

If you're on a team that doesn't have a single-step deployment strategy, find a time to talk with the project lead (or whoever), and see if they'll give you a day to try to get something set up.

Practice 12

Own Your Editor

I probably spend more time in my editor than I do in all the rest of the apps combined. It's where I code, where I write, where I take notes, and where I just tinker around.

I was an Emacs user for about 20 years. I loved its extensibility and liked the idea that it ran in a terminal, so I could use it anywhere, including over low-bandwidth remote connections. After a while I realized I was spending more time fiddling with my Emacs setup than I was getting work done.

For a while I used TextMate and then VS Code. Now I've gone back to the terminal, but this time with Vim (Neovim, to be accurate).

Cultivate Your Editor

Your editor is as personal to you as your own thoughts, adapting to your style, preferences, and workflow in ways that make it feel uniquely yours—at least it should be. I'm not going to intrude on that relationship by giving advice; I'm just going to describe some of the stuff I do.

Idea 31	**The shortest path from your brain to your code is your editor**

In the old days, I was a little out of control when it came to editing. I had thousands of lines of Emacs lisp that I'd written and probably tens of thousands of lines of extensions I'd downloaded. For a while I handled all my email, and read my newsgroups, directly in Emacs. But just because it's possible doesn't mean it's a good idea.

Over the years, I've trimmed down my editor setup as I've learned what I actually need and use. Switching to Vim was a great opportunity to work on this. I started with a totally vanilla installation of Neovim (via asdf) and then used it for a couple of days. At the end of that time, I had a list of things I wanted to do but couldn't. I spent 30 minutes researching and discovered that about 70 percent of these things were built into Vim already; I just didn't know how to access them. The rest were made possible by installing extensions. I added them one at a time, only adding the next after I'd learned the keystrokes I needed to be effective with the one I'd just installed.

As a Vim newbie, I watched a bunch of videos and read a lot of articles. Sometimes I'd come across something cool that I just had to install. I tried to have the discipline to uninstall it after I grew tired of the novelty.

I've been using Neovim for perhaps three years now. Here are the types of extensions I've settled on:

- A package manager
- Couple of nice dark themes
- LSP and Treesitter support for the languages I use
- Copilot support (normally disabled)
- An updated status line, including LSP and Git status information
- An extension that lets me align fields across a number of lines
- Multiple cursor support
- Something to show block nesting
- Support for navigation based on document syntax (uses Treesitter)
- Markdown preview

This short list covers pretty much everything I need.

Hate Those Meeses to Pieces

I also set myself the goal of not using a mouse while editing. I started by working out keyboard commands that helped me move around a buffer quickly, as this was my primary use of the mouse. While I'm still learning new tricks, I'm already way faster and more accurate than I was with a mouse, and my hands never leave the keyboard.

The next challenge was selecting text: making a selection with the mouse seemed so natural. But then I discovered Vim's text-objects. These allow you to apply a command to some semantic element in your file. If I just entered a function, and I'd like to format it, I just enter `v` `i` `f` `=` (which means visually select inside the current function and = (reformat....)). If I want to rewrap the lines in this paragraph, it's `v` `a` `p` `g` `q` (ap is all this paragraph and gq is [inexplicably] rewrap).

My last mouse dependency was selecting things such as file names from long lists. Fortunately Vim has a great fuzzy finder extension, so I just type A/Ed to open Automate/Editor.md.

And now I can say I'm mouse-free while editing. Interestingly, my right wrist no longer hurts at the end of the day.

Challenge

In your current editor, work out how to do the following:

- Reformat the body of an if statement, the current function, and the whole file.

- Set the column where text wraps to 75 and then rewrap your comments.

- Move the cursor to the start or end of the current function.

- Move the cursor to the opening brace corresponding to the closing brace it's on.

- Replace the single quotes around a string with double quotes.

- Return a count of the number of words in a Markdown document.

Challenge

Can you use your current editor without a mouse?

Explore

Just for kicks, try a different editor for any personal projects. Are there any ways it's better than your normal editor? Any ways it's worse?

Practice 13

Automate Setting Up Your Development Machine

Last week we had a thunderstorm, and some lightning struck our yard. It blew a few circuit breakers, but everything seemed to be OK...until I hit space and my Mac Mini didn't wake up. It turned out that although the power side was protected by my UPS, I have a long, unshielded Ethernet cable, and that must have picked up enough induced voltage to fry both the computer and the switch at the other end.

I took the computer to get it fixed, then dug out my laptop, which I haven't used for a while. I got it synced back to the state of the Mac Mini in about five minutes, including the new Vim configuration files, the changes I'd made to my terminal preferences, and all the repositories I'd been working on.

When I got the repaired computer back, it had been totally wiped. It took 40 minutes to go through the OS setup and about 20 minutes to install the base software I needed to create my environment. After that, I recovered my configuration and development files in a minute or two.

Idea 32	**Provision your development machine like it's a production server**

This recovery has two components: working files and configuration.

Working files are the easy part: just make sure they're under version control, and commit and push changes whenever you get to a point where you'd feel stupid if you lost the work you just did. I'd guess that 80 percent of my commit history is labeled "stash."

Recovering Tools and Configuration

Reinstalling the tools you use, along with their configurations, can be trickier.

One way to think about this is to treat your computer as being just another machine you deploy to—you are deploying your development environment, and not your app.

I know some developers who create their development environments in Docker containers. These contain the tools they need along with the configuration.

They then keep the actual project files in the host file system under version control. They save either the image or the Docker/Docker Compose scripts under version control. Provisioning a new laptop involves installing Docker or Podman, spinning up the containers, and then checking out the project files.

Hardcore developers use Nix to create and then re-create their environments. The benefit to this is that if you use Nix to install tools, it will already know what your environment should look like, so duplicating it on another machine should be easy.

I'm more primitive than these developers. I could definitely use Docker, but I don't. I could try to use Nix, but I was put off when I first spent a week trying to set it up a couple of years ago and just couldn't bend it to my will.

Instead, I use two tools to handle the applications and tools I install and one other app to handle my configuration.

Reinstalling Tools

The two application installers are asdf and Homebrew. asdf is mostly focused on tools directly associated with development, compilers, tools, and some editors. I like it because it makes it easy to run multiple versions of these tools on different projects without resorting to language-specific systems, such as Ruby's rbenv.

For the stuff that's not in asdf, I use Homebrew. It has great coverage, and application descriptions are actively maintained. It's not as good as asdf when it comes to project-local environments, though. (It can also be a little slow...)

Recovering Configuration

I have configuration files spread all over my file system. Some are in XDG directories, such as .config and .local. Others are in my home directory or in random places dictated by some app. I need to be able to save all of these under version control. Later, if I mess something up (or get a new machine), I need to be able to recover them, either singly or as a group.

A number of tools do this. Some people swear by GNU Stow, but I personally like yadm (Yet Another Dotfile Manager). This is a very thin wrapper around the Git command. It puts your whole hard drive under Git but then uses Git's *sparse checkout* facility so that it only manages the files you tell it to. You add files using yadm add, commit with yadm commit, push to GitHub or GitLab with yadm push, and restore to a new machine with yadm clone. It really is just Git for any file you nominate on your system. And, like Git, once you've added a file, it will track changes, so yadm status will tell you the files you've changed.

Remember to Track Your Tools

When talking about Homebrew and asdf, I skipped something important: how do I know which tools to install and what versions to use?

Idea 33	Track the tools you use as you install them

Fortunately both Homebrew and asdf have a way of recording their current configuration.

For Homebrew, I run brew bundle dump in my home directory; this creates a Brewfile. I can reinstall my current Homebrew setup by running brew bundle in that same directory.

asdf allows you to set both global and directly local dependencies. Things I use everywhere (such as the latest Ruby and Python) I set as global defaults. If I need a different Ruby in a particular project, I set it as a local default. These defaults are stored in files named .tool-versions. The global one is in my home directory, and the local ones are in each project's top-level directory. In any directory, you can type asdf install to install both the global and local tools.

I then add the files Brewfile and .tool-versions in my home directory to yadm. When I install on a fresh box, I just go to my home directory and type brew bundle and then asdf install.

Dumping the Homebrew configuration and updating yadm is managed by a cronjob that runs twice a day. The asdf side takes care of itself.

Cleaning House

To be honest, I wasn't too disappointed when my computer died. It's actually nice to be able to start afresh. Over time, my drive ends up full of random stuff that has become orphaned. With the new machine, I can load things back on as I need them. And, somehow, the tidier machine feels a little faster and a little less glitchy.

Thought

You start work this morning only to discover your computer has melted. Ignoring the somewhat worrying question of "what happened?" you're faced with getting productive on a new machine.

How long does it take you to get back to the state you were in at the end of the previous day?

Explore	

Do you know where the various configuration files are on your machine?

Try it	

If you have a laptop and a desktop, try installing something like yadm or stow on both. Initially create some dummy files on one of the machines; put them in different directories. Add them to yadm, commit, and push to a shared repo. On the other machine, clone that repo and verify the files you created have been installed in the correct places. Change the contents on one or more of them, check the status, and then commit them. Back on the first machine pull down the changes.

Really try it	

The next time you install an application that has configuration (an editor, perhaps), use a tool such as Homebrew, asdf, or Chocolatey. Then set up the app's initial configuration. Now save away all the information you'd need to reinstall and configure that app.

Then on the second machine, fetch the package manager list and configuration. Run the package manager to install the app and start it. You should see it using the same configuration you set up on the first machine.

CHAPTER 5

"Embrace Change"

Let's change tack; rather than developing code, let's look at developing *ourselves*.

How can we build our knowledge, skills, and career? How can we prepare for a future when that future is at best murky and uncertain?

When talking about software development, I recommended taking small steps—when we're not sure where we're going, a small step means we're less likely to fall off a cliff.

But that assumes we don't know what lies ahead. What if we could send out scouting parties? Like explorers mapping unknown terrain, they could scatter in different directions and return with valuable intelligence about what lies ahead. In software development, we call these scouting parties prototypes; in personal development, we call them research. And both prototypes and research make our decisions more confident and accurate.

Why?

If I was still doing what I did when I first started programming, I'd be punching Basic programs onto paper tape. To put it another way, I'd be unemployed.

Every developer knows this: of all the industries yet created, ours is probably the most volatile. For us, it's adapt and adopt—or perish. That's the pragmatic reason to do research.

But I strongly believe there's another reason. We developers are magicians; we conjure things out of our imagination—things that were previously not possible. And we do it, by and large, for the good of everyone. And, you know what? That's fun!

Idea 34 Software development is managed change

I've spent a lot of my life doing research. My family, bless them, call it *playing*. Maybe it is, and maybe that's why I do so much of it.

Learning something because you have to is a chore, but learning because you *want* to is a joy. For me, knowing that we live in a world where the pace of change has become scary is the driver, but being able to select to investigate things that look interesting or that glue together other things in novel ways—this is what drives me to want to learn.

The subtitle of Kent Beck's book *Extreme Programming [Bec00]* is *Embrace Change*. His philosophy is that teams who know how to rock and roll, adapting to changing environments, requirements, technologies, whatever—these teams will be more successful and will be at an advantage compared to their less flexible counterparts.

I don't want to put words into his mouth, but I'm sure he would feel that the same applies to people. In a world where the change curve appears to have gone exponential, we all have to find ways of coping. We need to find ways of tamping down the mild panic brought on by the feeling of drowning in the tsunami of the new. We all need to embrace change.

How can we do that? I think the answer, again, is to simplify the process. Structure it, and permit yourself to have fun with the new while continuing to use the tried and tested stuff in your work.

Here's what works for me.

Practice 14

Mix the Practical and the Fanciful

I get an immense amount of pleasure from seeing my software used.

But to experience that, I have to make sure that I have the skills I need to deliver in an increasingly sophisticated and demanding market.

This means I have two goals when I research. First, I need to find out about the technologies and techniques that are going to be useful to me. That's the *practical* part. Second, I need to understand which areas of development are the most rewarding for me personally. That's more fanciful.

Ponder...

- What areas of technology would be helpful in developing your career?

- And what areas of technology look interesting, outside a work context?

Here's how I'd answer those questions in 2025.

On the practical side, I need to know more about headless CMS systems, front-end frameworks, and edge services, as I'm planning for an upgrade to our site. I'm also looking at techniques for minimal downtime database migration and for less complex deployment options. Finally, I'm catching up on the latest developments in Rails and Phoenix.

> Idea 35 — **Research is what grownups call *play***

On the more fanciful side, here's what I'm playing with:

- *Microcontrollers.* ESP32 and the like, along with the cool sensors and displays now available.

- *Practical functional programming.* I keep looking for a pure functional language that I can love.

- *Algebraic effects.* These are a way of isolating side effects in functional languages. They exist to solve the same problem that monads solve, but in (I feel) a much tidier way.

- *The Unison language.* A functional language (with algebraic effects) that also has the idea of immutable code. Immutable code means no more package management, and you can deploy your app by sending a 512-bit checksum to a server.

Research Is a Valid Activity

It's easy to think that research is something you do in your spare time. When I fall into that trap, two things happen. First, I never have spare time, and as a result I never really play, because I feel guilty.

Idea 36	**All work and no play makes Dave a grumpy boy**

After a period of not playing, though, the pressure builds until I just have to do some research. By then, the list of things I want to look at has grown to the point where I find myself skipping around between them, never really getting deep enough to earn a real return.

So set aside time for research. It might be 20 minutes a day, or three hours one evening—whatever fits with your life and the way you learn. For me, I like to do it either in the mornings, for 30 minutes after I've handled email, or at night; I do a fair amount of reading in bed...

To make it effective, I jot down my goal for each session. This can be as simple as "Write a distributed Unison program" or "How does server-side rendering affect deployment?" or "What's José Valim up to?"

Then I set about trying to meet that goal. Because it's too easy to skim through stuff and get distracted, I keep my daybook open and jot down notes. If I come across some other area that looks interesting, I write it down and circle it; I'll come back to it in a future session, but I won't derail this session's objectives.

I Allow Myself Some Playtime

Although I try to focus my research on practical things, I also give myself time to do things just for the hell of it. Sometimes it's just reading, but more often it involves code. I'm forever writing little explorations of ideas, just to see how they come out. I also like messing around with hardware: my favorite of these projects was the conversion of a Fisher Price Classic Pull-A-Tune Xylophone into a touch-sensitive midi controller, courtesy of a Raspberry Pi. Somewhere in my office there's a Teddy Ruxpin bear that's been beefed up with servos that respond to the sounds from digital recordings. Along the way, I learned a lot about sound processing, low-level networking, and how not to manipulate plastic.

Idea 37   Use it or lose it

Once I've learned something, and if it's appropriate, I try to find a way to knock up a quick prototype, just to double-check I actually understood it. It'll be ugly code, but that doesn't matter, because I'll delete it when I'm done. Again, I'll jot down notes in my daybook about the things I learned along the way.

Plan your research

Try to make two lists, each three items long. The first is the list of things that you really should know more about; the second is the list of things you're curious about.

Set aside some regular time for research and start working through the lists. Initially, try alternating: do a "should do" entry, then do a "fun to do" entry.

As you're researching, add new things that catch your attention to the appropriate list.

And remember to keep notes.

Practice 15

Play in the Future, Work in the Past

Maybe it's just me, but whenever I come across something new and interesting, I want to roll it into my next project. It's fresh, it has some new ideas, and I want to get experience using it for real.

I've learned the hard way that this is a bad idea. New technologies tend to change quickly, and I can spend more time migrating my code between releases than I spend coding.

New things have more bugs than old things. They may have worse documentation, less in the way of online support, fewer extensions, a scarcity of tutorials, and so on.

The Roman God Janus, who faced both the past and the future

More insidiously, I fall prey to a new idea when it solves some particular problem I'm stuck on. The bright shiny new thing may well solve that problem. But often it fails to solve other problems that my old software handled well, so I'm left trying to glue the old and the new into a kind of Frankenproject.

It took me a long time to get control of my magpie tendencies—to stop collecting shiny trinkets and instead to plod along with my old, familiar (and working) tools. When it comes to the tools and libraries you rely on every day, boring trumps exciting every time.

This is where dedicating time to research pays off. I know that I'll be able to play with all these new things during that time, which makes working with the familiar the rest of the time easier to bear. Here's where the daybook comes in handy. When I find myself wondering if maybe, just maybe, it would be OK to use Rails 29.32-beta on my new project, because the rewrite in PHP looks interesting, I instead just write a note in my daybook and continue along the path more traveled. I know that, if I'm still interested, I'll be able to play with Rails in an upcoming research session.

Research Dave is an advance scout, finding out what lies ahead for his alter-ego, Production Dave.

Think back...

Consider your past projects. Have they ever been made more difficult because you or your team chose to use bleeding-edge libraries, frameworks, or tools?

In the end, did these things live up to their promise? Did they make a difference to the value that you delivered that was worth the extra stress?

Pair research

If other people on your team also keep lists of things to research, why not compare notes? If two (or more) of you want to look into (say) OCAML, you could join forces and turn it into a social thing as well as a tech thing. My bet is that you'll learn more per unit time.

Part III

Simplify Your Interactions

CHAPTER **6**

Soft Skills

Writing this chapter is a bit of a penance for me; of all the things in this book, these are the areas I personally need to work on the most.

To some people, these things come naturally. If you're one of these people, you may find some of the ideas here a little obvious (but you're probably too nice to mention it). But if, like me, you know you can do better, perhaps my experiences will help.

Why You Should Care

In the old days, a single super-programmer could design and code an entire project, keeping most of the details in their head.

Those days are (for the most part) long in the past. Today, software is written by teams. And teams are formed of people, and people are influenced by opinions, emotions, and fear. Working in a team can be incredibly rewarding. It can also be a minefield, when one false step can ruin your day.

What Does This Have to Do with Simplicity?

Friction is wasted effort. In a gearbox, that waste becomes heat. In a team, it is frustration and wasted time. Without trust and clear communication, things that should be simple to express become way more complicated, and misunderstandings are rife. It's hard to make things simple when you can't trust they are correctly understood.

So let's look at some ways we can navigate through the minefield, taking more confident and less stressful steps.

Practice 16

Disagreements Are Not Zero-Sum Games

One of the problems of our times is that people are convinced that the only way they can win is for someone else to lose. Couple that with the fact that many people care more about winning than about the actual longer-term outcome, and you end up with a dysfunctional and noisy world.

A simple difference of opinion can end up as a confrontation. Some people like that, and others walk away. Neither side actually wins in that situation.

Idea 38   No one wins a zero-sum argument

An alternative approach is to realize that things are rarely black and white. No one is likely to be 100 percent right about anything. The trick is to accept this and to make what would otherwise have been an argument into something more like an exploration.

This approach is called *dialectical reasoning*. It assumes there are elements of truth in both sides of an opinion, and it emphasizes the benefits of trying to synthesize something new and bigger from them. Just as important, it turns something that threatened to be a confrontation into an interesting discussion.

Practice dialectical thinking

Here's the exercise. The next time you find yourself disagreeing with someone, try not to flip the bozo bit and assume they're an idiot. Rather than trying to show them they are wrong, instead genuinely try to work out if maybe you are. Be actively interested in what led them to their position, not because you're hoping to trip them up, but rather because it might give you insights. Your mission is not to prove you're correct or that the other person is wrong. Instead, you are trying to find out which parts of each of your positions have merit and from that synthesize a new understanding that's better than the two original ones.

This is tricky; it's easy to come across as condescending or maybe sly. You might start by saying, "I hear what you are saying, but I need to understand more about Xyz because it doesn't quite line up with my experience. Could you show me what led to your belief."

Never disagree; you're not trying to win. The exercise is to see things from their point of view. A nice side effect might be that you end up learning something.

Arguing with knives

Here's a fun exercise that helps you practice seeing things from both sides. Next time you're at a lunch or dinner where half the people advocate one thing and the other half advocate the opposite, suggest the following game.

Everyone who agrees with the position should place their knives (or spoons, or pens, or…) pointing into the center of the table (the way a knife is normally set). Those who disagree should place their knives at 90º to this, parallel to the edge of the table.

Let the debate run for a few minutes. Then pick a pair of people who disagree and flip their knives around; the person who previously advocated for the position must now argue against it, and the person who previously refuted it must now do their best to sell it to everyone else.

Keep swapping a pair of knives every few minutes. Try to give everyone a chance to cycle through both sides of the issue more than once.

It becomes a game: how can you marshal what you know to support something you disagree with. It's like high school debate.

You're not trying to find winners or losers, or even to find a consensus. It's just an interesting way to spend 30 minutes with friends.

But on the way home, you might just find yourself reevaluating some of your strongly held views.

Idea 39   Absolute is the enemy of simple

You might be wondering what this has to do with simplicity.

Think of someone you know who 100 percent believes in something. How much energy do they have to put in to sustain that belief in the face of evidence to the contrary? How much time do they waste making decisions on the basis of things that are only partially true.

A team run on absolutes is never going to be efficient. They'll find it much harder to change when the world changes. And they'll be missing out on the better ideas that come from synthesizing varieties of viewpoints.

Work On Your Empathy

If you work on just one soft skill, work on empathy.

Let's start with a definition: *empathy is the ability to understand how another person feels and to take that into account when dealing with them.* It doesn't mean you have to agree with them—just that you have to consider and respect them and their positions.

Empathy acts as a social lubricant, allowing people to reach mutually satisfactory decisions. As soon as two or more people work together, they need to find a way to share what they know, what they believe, and what they plan. The more efficiently and effectively they can do this, things become simpler, and work becomes more agile.

Think of the long-term couples you know. Watch them communicate and resolve problems with nothing more than some gestures and the occasional eye contact.

Now think about talking with a customer about a new project. If you try to see *their* problems through *their* eyes as well as your own, you'll be in a far better position to produce technical solutions that deliver what that customer actually needs and not just what they say they want. You'll also be able to explain that solution in terms they understand.

When you have empathy with others, you can short-circuit a lot of trial and error. You can take smaller steps because you know they'll trust you. If you mess up, you know that others will understand your frustration and regret rather than blame you. You feel freer to experiment when you have that emotional safety net.

Another way of thinking about the link between empathy and simplicity is to consider what happens when there's no empathy. People look out for themselves and protect their own ideas and plans against dilution from other people's input. Work becomes siloed, and decisions tend to become absolute. Organizations will tend to become more hierarchical because that makes it easier to preserve authority. The reaction to setbacks is not learning—it's blame. Perhaps this sounds familiar?

Although empathy is all about groups of people, it is up to each individual to find their own path to expressing and using it. Then it's about the team accepting and amplifying each person's interactions.

If the scale goes from 10 being totally empathetic to 0 being Ted Bundy, I'm probably a 4. But since doing the research for this book, I've realized that's not good enough, so I'm venturing out of my comfort zone and working on developing empathy.

Here are some of the things I'm trying or plan to try.

Give People Time

In some ways, time is our most limited resource. We live with constant time pressure and feel guilty if we're not being productive.

This is one of my biggest problems when dealing with people. I view my work interactions as transactional—some kind of information exchange. I try to get them done efficiently, then move on.

That is wrong. Each time I do this I erode my connection with the other person; I treat them as a resource and not a human being.

So my personal exercise, which I recommend to you if you're like me, is to make the transaction secondary to the overall interaction. Make time for the person and not just for the information. Try not to look like you want to rush off to put out the next fire—enjoy being with another human for a few minutes.

One thing I've noticed as I try to get better at this: it seems to be a lot easier to practice with people you don't know. Another trick is to have some generic questions you can use to get them chatting. They call it small talk, but it's really the glue that binds tribes together. All it takes is taking the time to listen.

Idea 40	Small talk is about listening, not talking

What we're learning here is to see things from other people's points of view. Being able to chat comfortably with someone means you care enough to remember things about them and their life.

How Do I Look to Others?

I'm English. I was raised to wear my heart in a hermetically sealed Kevlar-lined box that I keep in a floor safe under the bed.

It doesn't matter whether I'm upset, frustrated, bored, concentrating, pleased—however I'm feeling, I'm always surprised that people don't seem to notice. I don't tell people I have a bad toothache; I expect them to work it out. Then I'm disappointed when my clipped answers to their questions annoy them.

If you believe that how you feel is obvious, then are you ever surprised when people don't correctly assess your mood? If you feel that maybe it isn't so obvious, are you sometimes hurt that people just don't get how you're feeling?

Either way, what could we do to make it easier for people to know what we're feeling without also going off the deep end?

Personally, I'm trying to tell people if I'm feeling something strongly. I try not to make it sound like it's all about me, but when I realize that I've been curt with someone, I might add on "I'm sorry. That probably sounded terse. I've got a bad tooth, and I'm finding it hard to concentrate."

Idea 41	**Don't assume people know how you feel; tell them**

If people misinterpret how you're feeling, then it's a safe bet you've done the same to them on occasion. So how can you find out how they really feel?

Try this

People get very tired of someone who's constantly asking if they feel upset. But there are other ways of asking that actually make people feel good:

"Hi, Jan! What're you up to?"
"I've just spent the morning tracking down a bug in the report formatter."
"Ouch! That kind of thing can be really frustrating."
"Actually, I quite enjoy it."
"Really? Why's that…"

Make a game of it: periodically try to assess someone's mood by just observing them and then try to find a way of asking them without directly asking the question.

Do I Have Power?

Sometimes, with all the daily frustrations, it's easy to forget that we developers have a surprising amount of power. We make things happen. We understand both the real world and the abstract world of schemas and architectures. Quite often, we know more about the overall business than just about anyone else in the company.

This often places us on the privileged side of an interaction. We have the option to lord it over the other person, to wield our arcane knowledge to make ourselves feel special and powerful. We can score points.

And, unfortunately, we often get away with it, because the rest of the world just shrugs and thinks "programmers, eh? Sad…"

Try this

If you find yourself in a situation where you are scoring points by showing off your godlike knowledge of something, change the rules. The new game is that you score whenever you get the other person to understand a point you're making well enough that they paraphrase it back to you.

It Works Up the Chain, Too…

One of the strange aspects of the software business is that developers actually have a lot of power over their managers. This is one cause of friction: the managers may (tacitly) feel the need to exert control to stop their charges from getting out of hand.

So practice empathy when talking with them. Take away the feeling that you're some kind of threat and make them feel better about themselves by the end of every conversation.

Practice the Golden Rule

John Stuart Mill phrased it, "to do as you would be done by." Treat others the way you'd hope they would treat you. Being nice is a positive-sum game.

The common interpretation of this is "don't be a jerk." But there's another, far more positive aspect.

Try this

As an exercise, spend a month proactively doing nice, unsolicited things for people. Nothing dramatic, but things that show that you've thought about what someone else would want. Fetch your desk neighbor a cup of coffee when you refill yours. Make a point of telling a colleague how good their latest PR looked. Offer to finish off running the tests for them if a teammate needs to leave a little early to pick up their kid.

This exercise has two benefits. First, it makes you think about other people and what they might need. That's empathy right there.

The other benefit is that things will feel nicer. You'll feel good being nice to folks, and they'll feel appreciated.

Empathy Is Anticipated Feedback

I believe that empathy has a core role to play in making things simple. Empathy is a way of gathering essential feedback on ourselves; we imagine a situation from someone else's viewpoint and use that to adjust our behavior.

This lets us move a lot faster and with less friction. We could just do something mindlessly and then handle the reaction. But if we misjudged the situation, we'd have all that work to undo, and all that trust to rebuild. It's not very efficient.

But two or more people who have empathy can bypass a lot of that: they can respond to nonverbal cues and to anticipated needs to make lots of smaller decisions and to try them out both implicitly and explicitly. Working with empathy means getting pretty much instantaneous feedback and making continuous minute corrections. And that makes things a lot simpler.

How well do you know each other?

The Johari Window is an exercise to help you discover how your view of yourself agrees with other people's view of you. As well as providing often surprising differences between your opinion of yourself and that of others, the exercise also helps you explore things that you might want to open up about as a way of building trust. You can find plenty of information online.[1] If you want to try it, I'd recommend having someone who's not participating run the session, just to keep things on an even keel.

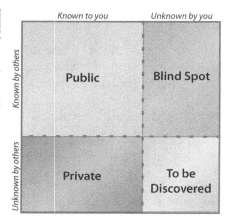

---

1.   https://www.mindtools.com/au7v71d/the-johari-window

Have Empathy for Things

Everyone has a relative who has a *might-makes-right* approach to the physical world. If a key doesn't turn in a lock, turn it harder until it breaks off. If the car won't start, run the battery flat trying to force it to. If the jar won't open, bend the tip of your favorite knife trying to pry it. (Do I sound a little bitter? I liked that knife...)

These people seem to lack the ability (or will) to think of themselves as part of a system, where the physical thing they're working on has its own constraints and preferred way of doing things. They don't think, "Could this be the wrong key? Maybe it's upside down?" or "Why doesn't the car start? What am I forgetting?" or "What other way do jars open? Should I try twisting the top?"

| Idea 42 | **Understand your environment; don't fight it** |

Empathy for people means experiencing things from their perspective, understanding how they work, what they can do, and what their limits are. Physical things lack an inner perspective, but they do have ways of working, things they can do, and limits.

Knowing and acting on this is a form of empathy and, just as with social empathy, learning to use it makes things easier and simpler.

A long time ago I had a share of a sailboat. My co-owner and I did alright, but we knew we'd benefit from some training, so we had an experienced skipper sail with us for a weekend. It was humbling. When we sailed, we steered by forcing the helm back and forth. We trimmed sails by loosening or tightening sheets a foot at a time. Sailing was tiring. When our experienced skipper sailed, he barely moved. He had his fingers resting on the helm, and steered by gently curling and uncurling them, often imperceptibly. He'd trim the sails once, and then adjust the sheets as needed, and by inches.

He didn't fight the boat, trying to bend it to his will. Instead, he felt the boat and came to an agreement with it. He had empathy, used less energy, and the boat ran faster and more smoothly. He made sailing simple.

Listen to Your Code

This is what it's like when you start listening to your code. You'll find yourself making small adjustments without really being aware of it. Simple.

But just how do you listen to your code?

How often do you feel uneasy with a function as you're writing it or look at a screen of code and think, "Something's wrong," before you even consciously read the characters? Do you ever feel your code pushing back as you write it; you can't stop thinking, "This is harder than it should be"?

The trick is to recognize this and to work on doing something when the feeling surfaces.

A good place to start is when debugging. We all know people who are good at it. Their trick is that they stop thinking of the bug as a mistake. Instead, the bug is simply the system doing what it was told to do. They stop looking for the code that is wrong. Instead, they look at the system as a whole and ask, "What could make it respond like that?" They think about the flows of data and control and wonder how they can isolate segments of both. They're treating the system the same way a diagnostician treats a patient.

If you sometimes struggle when debugging, try switching perspectives. Think about the poor code, forced by some mistake to behave badly. What might cause it to do that? How can you ask it questions to better understand what it's doing? I know it sounds a little new-agey, but it works for me.

Taking it a step beyond debugging, start looking for your subconscious giving you warnings about your work. The symptoms are often subtle:

- You leave your desk to get a drink more often than usual.
- You keep renaming things.
- You feel like typing is hard work.
- You want to stop and do something else.
- And other avoidance behaviors.

I met the person who'd become my wife in New York. She had lived there for a while; I was a visitor.

When we walked down the street, she'd sometimes hip check me toward the street. After a while, I asked why she was doing this, and she said she wasn't. The next time it happened, I stopped dead and showed her I'd been moved.

After that, we worked out that whenever she passed a passage or doorway where someone could be hiding, she stepped away. This wasn't conscious. It was a reflex.

The Gift of Fear

Gavin de Becker's company provides personal protection for people who are targets for acts of aggression. He wrote an amazing book, *The Gift of Fear [de 97]*, in which he describes what those of us who can't afford a bodyguard can do to avoid danger.

One piece of advice has stuck with me over the years since I read it: learn to trust your instincts. He claims that most people who are mugged on the street report that they felt uneasy before the attack happened but just shrugged it off.

The feeling of being uneasy is your subconscious recognizing patterns that you might not be aware of. It might have noticed a shadow move or heard breathing or soft footsteps. It has no way to tell your conscious brain, "Hey! Watch out!" So instead it triggers lower-level responses: your heart rate may increase, you might feel a little queasy or cold. And he helps his clients learn to recognize and act on these feelings.

His point is that these reflexes helped us survive in more primitive times. Ignoring them now means throwing away thousands of years of collective experience, along with dozens of years of your own.

Listen to your lizard brain

The next time you feel strange, when things feel a little off, try not to shrug it off. Instead, examine that feeling. What were you doing when it started? What is it making you feel?

Here's a trick that might work for you. You know how people say that often they get their best ideas in the shower or when walking? These are times when their conscious brain is idling, and this gives their subconscious room to break through.

So when my spidey-sense fires, and I can't immediately put my finger on the cause, I take a break. Sometimes I walk, or start to doodle, or do some tidying. Often, the thing that triggered the incident just pops into my head.

Perhaps that might work for you.

Practice 19

Spin a Story

Your boss's boss steps into the elevator. "You work on the back-end stuff, don't you?" You nod and smile. "So maybe you can tell me: why am I paying for four times the amount of storage than we need to hold our data?"

You think for a second: "Oh, it's the extra space we need for all the indexes."

"So what's an index, and why am I paying for it?"

Now this is a question you can answer.

> An index is a mapping between the values in one or more columns in a relationship to the row or rows that contain those values. The index is hashed or sorted to make access fast, and once you find a value in an index, you can get straight to the rows with those values in the given columns.

You stop talking and smile. This was just like a job interview—you aced it.

So you're somewhat surprised when your boss's boss (boss[2]) scowls, mutters something about gibberish, and gets off the next time the doors open.

You gave a great, factual answer. And you communicated nothing.

Let's rewind and replay the scene, but this time with a version of you that has practiced the ideas in this section.

Take Two

"So what's an index, and why am I paying for it?"

You stop to think. Your boss[2] is smart but not technical. You know the answer to their question is that the indexes take up space, but how can you explain why the indexes are needed. You need a story—an analogy.

> Well, our systems need to be able to find one particular piece of information out of the billions of things we store. To do that they create indexes. An index is just like the index in a book: you can search it quickly, and then it takes you right to the page you want. We have to look up things in lots of different ways, so we have lots of indexes. And just like the index in a book takes up space, our indexes take up space, too.

As you've been weaving this tale, you've been watching boss^2's face. They've been nodding, and their eyes never left you. At the end, they smile. "Ah, that makes total sense. I wish your boss could explain things to me like that."

Fiction, Not Friction

You might be thinking that the story is not accurate. Database indexes are way more complex than that, and they're constantly reorganizing themselves, something the average physical index rarely does. You made yourself look like you don't know even the simplest thing about database internals.

So what?

In this situation—in most situations—your task is to convey information, to communicate. To do that, you need to think about the circumstances:

- What information is important in context?
- What vocabulary will be effective communicating it?
- Are there analogies or metaphors that map the information onto that vocabulary?
- Will any information that is lost or misrepresented by the analogy affect the listener's understanding?

Let's apply this to the elevator conversation about indexes.

What information is important in context?
> You want to explain that the total amount of storage is more than the amount of underlying data because your applications use many indexes.

What vocabulary will be effective communicating it?
> You know that boss^2 won't follow (or be interested) in hearing about hashing and B-trees, so you want to spin a nontechnical tale.

Are there analogies or metaphors that map the information onto that vocabulary?
> You try to come up with some real-world example where data is indexed and those indexes take up space. A book index is an obvious analog.

Will any information that is lost or misrepresented by the analogy affect the listener's understanding?
> You quickly work through the idea, remembering that all you need to explain is that indexes make access faster but take up space. Your story gets that across, so it's good enough.

A good analogy illustrates what you need to communicate in a language that speaks to your listener. It won't be the whole truth, and it may even be inaccurate in the details.

Idea 43   Analogies are useful lies

A 100 percent accurate low-level answer will cause friction unless the listener is as familiar as you are with all the details. A mostly accurate analogy or metaphor trades away that friction at the risk of introducing a little fiction.

Choosing a Domain

One of the hardest parts of this kind of storytelling is choosing the domain—the world where your story lives. It's difficult because it has to be rich enough to convey your message, but at the same time it must be easily understood by both you and your listener.

For this reason, you should probably only use this technique if you and your listener share common backgrounds.

Here are some things to avoid.

Areas where only one of you has deep knowledge
> You may be a baseball fanatic, but explaining something by drawing a parallel to the infield fly rule will fall flat unless your listener shares your passion.

> Also avoid using domains where your listener is knowledgeable and you are not. If you know your listener is an avid opera goer, don't try using *The Marriage of Figaro* as a metaphor for key exchange algorithms unless you also love Mozart.

Politics, religion, social issues, and the like
> Duh.

Worlds that take a long time to establish
> People looking for information won't tolerate a 15-minute introduction to the characters and mores of the analogy. You have to pick something that requires almost no background information.

Topical personalities or social media happenings
> Surprisingly not everyone follows *#mycatatethemailman*.

Instead, look for worlds that you share—classic movies, practical life experiences, quirks of your office network, the weather. If you could use it to make small talk with someone, it's probably fair game.

This Is Empathy in Action

When we come up with stories to explain unfamiliar concepts, what we're really doing is seeing the situation from the other person's perspective. We imagine what it would feel like to have someone answer what seems to be a simple question with a bunch of incomprehensible jargon; it would make the recipient feel intimidated, ignorant, frustrated, or just plain angry.

So, instead, we use our empathy to create a way of mapping our world into theirs.

The Essence of Analogy

Before we dig into the art of creating stories, let's look at why analogies work.

We're trying to explain something that is outside our listener's comfort zone. The thing we're trying to explain has a number of different components, and those components interact in a predictable way. The problem is that our listener doesn't know any of this. So we come up with a different domain, one that the listener does understand, and map each of the components in our original description into corresponding components in the analogy's domain.

A good analogy contains more, though. We're trying to illustrate how the thing we're describing works in the real world—how its real-world components will interact and produce results. For the analogy to be effective, the corresponding components in the analogy's domain must also interact, and that interaction must produce a result that maps back to the real world.

In our index example, here's what this look like:

The index enables very fast lookup of something in a book.
   The database index enables very fast lookup of the location of some data.

The indexes take space in the book.
   The database indexes take storage space.

The more indexes you have, the more ways you can look something up.
   The more database indexes, the more ways you can rapidly find data.

The more indexes you have, the more space they take.
   The more database indexes you have, the more storage they take.

Is the mapping perfect? Not at all. Possibly the biggest inaccuracy is that the space overhead of a book index is considerably less that the overhead of database indexes. It also skips all the database-level stuff that indexes can do. None of that matters, though; the analogy is accurate enough to help us communicate our point. That's all we need.

Creating the Analogy

Probably the simplest way to come up with an analogy is to look at the names of the things you're trying to explain. In the database example, we wanted to talk about records and indexes. The word *index* suggested book, and it didn't take too much thought to go from there.

Let's look at another example. You're managing an application which sells event tickets. Under peak load, you're suffering from performance issues caused by contention for database locks. Your (nontechnical) manager wants to know why you can't just add a dozen more servers to fix the problem.

Use the checklist to help come up with an analogy.

What information is important in context?
> The issue is not the ability to handle the initial incoming request. Instead, it's caused by every request having to queue up to write to the database at the end of processing. We need to explain that extra processing power outside the database won't help.

What vocabulary will be effective communicating it?
> We're looking at a situation when incoming events can initially be processed in parallel but that eventually have to queue to get exclusive access to some resource. The word *queue* immediately triggers a rich set of scenarios—everyone has spent time waiting in queues.

Are there analogies or metaphors that map the information onto that vocabulary?
> We could describe the process of checking in with bags at an airport. Passengers first hand their bags over to the airline and then line up to pass through the security checkout. The interaction where they dump their bags is like the initial processing of a request in our system, and waiting for their turn in the security line is equivalent to queuing for the database.

Will any information that is lost or misrepresented by the analogy affect the listener's understanding?
> I think we have a good enough match to start spinning a yarn.

"I understand why you'd like to throw some more hardware at the handling of our incoming requests. Here's why we don't think it will be as effective as we want.

"Imagine our system is like a train station. Passengers arrive and buy a ticket, just like our users. They find a free ticket machine and buy a ticket. Those machines are like the servers that handle incoming requests. They then have to join the line to pass through security checks. They can only do this one at a time. That's the same as our requests waiting to update the database.

"Everyone complains about how long it takes to get to their train. We might think that we should add more ticket machines, so we can handle more arriving passengers in parallel. That won't help, because people will still end up waiting at security.

"Instead, we need to focus our attention on the security bottleneck. What can we do to get people through it faster? Run more lanes in parallel? Cut down on the number of interactions with each person? Speed up the processing of each passenger?

"That's why we think that our time is better spent looking at the database bottleneck."

I think this is a pretty good analogy: the concepts in the real world (our application, request handling, and database contention) map well into the analogy (train station, ticket machine, and security). Interactions in the real world are modeled by corresponding interactions in the story, and as a result the conclusions we can draw from the analogy apply in the real world, too.

Idea 44	**Concepts in the story should interact like their real-world counterparts**

Performance Anxiety

It's difficult to come up with good analogies on the spot. I can't count the number of times I've finished a frustrating conversation only to come up with the ideal analogy on the trip home.

But it *is* possible to practice, and with practice comes the ability to think on your feet. Here are three ideas:

Practice offline storytelling

You don't have to be face-to-face with someone to use stories. In fact, it's a lot easier to do it asynchronously.

Email is a great way of practicing your technique without the stress of having to respond immediately.

When questions arrive in your inbox, pause before you answer, and ask yourself what the sender actually needs and how you could best explain it. Maybe use the checklist as an *aide-mémoire*.

Write your response using an analogy and then add something like "I'm not sure if I explained that clearly. Did it make sense?" Feedback in all things…

Practice social storytelling

We've all been in this situation: your aunt comes over and asks you (again) just what is it you do. Or your uncle wants to know "what the hell is an SSID?"

You'll never have a friendlier audience to practice on. You can even tell them, "I'm working on finding new ways to explain things. Do you mind being a guinea pig?" And then give it your best shot. Ask them if you're making sense as you go along.

Of course the downside of this is that you'll become the go-to source for every technical question in your family.

Take an improv class

I've been to a couple of conferences that offered the opportunity of spending an afternoon with improv comedians, learning and practicing some of their techniques. It was interesting to see how some attendees blossomed as the afternoon progressed (I was not one of them). But even the worst of us learned useful techniques ("yes, and…") for buying some thinking time while keeping a conversation going.

Tell Yourself Stories, Too

I often find myself trying to write some software when I don't fully understand what I need to do. Normally I'd write throwaway prototypes to explore various solutions. But I've also found it useful to spend a few minutes trying to come up with an analogy for the problem I'm trying to solve. Once I'm thinking in the domain of the story, I might see how those fictional objects might interact to achieve their (fictional) outcome. Sometimes I can then map that action back into my problem domain.

Ask yourself

Come up with some analogies to help answer the following technical questions for one of your friends who isn't that technical.

1. How does a stack (or a LIFO queue) work?
2. How does a FIFO queue work?
3. Just what *is* an SSID?
4. What's the difference between a computer's memory and storage?

Part IV

Simplify Your Code

This part is something of an anomaly. The other parts are fairly high level, but here I dive down into the code.

It's also strange because its two chapters are very different. The first is an exploration of using data to drive the operation of code rather than have code simply process data. The chapter is there not because it's the only way of simplifying code, but because as a technique it is easy to implement, it delivers a lot of benefit, and it isn't widely used.

The second chapter in this part is even stranger: it's a collection of one- or two-page very low-level practices that I use daily when coding.

A lot of debate surrounded whether to include this part. The last thing I want to do is tell you how to code. In the end it's included because I think it illustrates a way of thinking about the mechanics of coding—looking for simplifications whenever you bump into something that gets in your way.

## CHAPTER 7

Data Driven

I used to think my job as a programmer was to write code that manipulated data—inputs became outputs, data became information. My programs were structured fairly imperatively, even when writing in OO or functional languages, because my implicit assumption was that the code was in charge.

I was wrong, of course. The code is not in charge—it's simply one tool we use to deliver value.

I now have a different view of development, and one that makes my code simpler. The effective approach to programming is to have data and code hand control back and forth. Sometimes code generates data; sometimes data drives the code.

The benefit of this is clear: data is easier to work with than code. It's easier to reason about, easier to manipulate, and easier to change. The more you drive your code with data, the more your code inherits these attributes, too.

Idea 45	**Data is simpler than code**

Every application is already driven by the data it receives as input; those values affect conditional code and loops. But here I'm talking about a deeper layer of data—data that is part of the logic of the application.

This can be done in many, many ways. In this chapter I look at two: using tables to sequence the execution of code and then taking the idea further with state machines.

These concepts are just the tip of the iceberg. An application's configuration is also data that controls its behavior. The way we supply and update that data can either simplify our apps or make them more complicated.

Data in transit between parts of an application can also drive what happens next.

We can take it further, using data structures to control what and when code gets executed. This is a great way of simplifying tests.

For real control, we can turn to state machines; they're not as complicated as people make them out to be, and they're a great way of turning deeply nested code into nice linear chunks.

You'll be amazed just how much simpler your code can become by making parts of it data driven.

Practice 20

Let the Data Do the Driving

Replacing code with data is probably at the top of the list of things that give me that self-satisfied feel-good feeling when I code.

I love taking code that is either repetitive or close to being repetitive and shrinking it all down to a single function that can be parameterized by data.

Why? Because...

| Idea 46 | **Data is easier to change than code** |

Maybe I'm creating a bunch of shapes for a drawing program:

```
shape = add_shape(Triangle, sides: 3)
shapes_by_sides[3].push(shape)

shape = add_shape(Square, sides: 4)
shapes_by_sides[4].push(shape)

shape = add_shape(Rhombus, sides: 4)
shapes_by_sides[4].push(shape)
   :                    :
```

I'd most likely write the code this way when I start with the first shape and stick with this structure when I add the second. But by the third, I'm thinking that I need to separate the data that changes from the code that doesn't.

```
[
  [ Triangle, 3 ],
  [ Square,   4 ],
  [ Rhombus,  4 ],
     :
].forEach(([ cls, sides ]) => {
  let shape = add_shape(cls, sides: sides)
  shapes_by_sides[sides].push(shape)
})
```

I know—this code is slightly longer than the original, but despite that I think it's simpler for two related reasons:

1. It makes the list of shapes explicit so that it's easier to scan and to maintain.

2. It separates two different ideas: a list of shapes and the code that adds each shape to our system. In the initial example code, all this was jumbled together.

Now, adding a new shape just means adding a new line to the table.

Managing Method Chains with Error Handling

Now we need to handle geometric transformations on our shapes. Each of the transform functions returns a tuple: [status, new_shape]. If the status is ok, then new_shape will contain a new, transformed version of the shape, otherwise an error occurred, and the new_shape value is invalid.

```
let square = new Square(10)

let [ status, square1 ] = scale(square, 0.5)
if (status == "ok") {
  let [ status, square2 ] = rotate(square1, -5)
  if (status == "ok") {
    let [ status, square3 ] = skew(square2, 0.1)
    if (status == "ok") {
      display(square3)
    }
  }
}
```

We've all written code like this. But we can make it data driven and flatten it out:

```
const transform = [
  (shape) => scale(shape, 0.5),
  (shape) => rotate(shape, -5),
  (shape) => skew(shape, 0.1),
]
let square = new Square(10)
for (let cmd of transform) {
  [ status, shape ] = cmd(shape)
  if (status != "ok") {
    shape = undefined
    break
  }
}
if(shape)
  display(shape)
```

It's harder to assert that the data-driven code is simpler in this example, but I'm going to try. :)

First, this example is pretty trivial. In the real world, the nested code tends to be more complex and often deeper. The benefits are clearer in these cases.

Even in this simple case, though, the data-driven approach achieves a number of things:

- We've separated the specification of the sequence of transforms from the code that does the transforming, making it easier to see what's going on and to change it. (Compare the ease of swapping the order of the scale and skew transforms in each example.)

- Because this transformation specification is now just a value, we can use it in other places.

- We've replaced the nesting with a loop. In languages that support an interruptible reduce function, we could even replace the loop as well.

- We can now test the transforms individually.

> **Idea 47**   **The data is the *what* and the code is the *how***

Data-Driven Code Is an Interpreter

I've said for a long time that people should write code by writing interpreters, and I've become used to the "yeah, sure" look that follows. I now realize I needed to explain it better. When I said "interpreter," people imagined the massive and complicated environments that execute programming languages like Java, Ruby, Python, or Elixir. But interpreters don't have to be complex.

An interpreter is simply code that is told what to do by some data. In the case of programming languages, that data may be in the form of a syntax tree or bytecode, and the interpreter is the code that scans that data and performs actions based on it.

Our previous example of shape drawing is an interpreter: the data is the table of shape names and sides, and the execution part is the loop that runs through this table, invoking the appropriate actions.

Simple interpreters such as this are a key strategy when it comes to making things easy to change. (They also make the code easier to write in the first place.)

Driven by External Data

All the examples so far have used literal values in the code itself to define the data that drives the code execution. That's not a requirement. The data can be dynamic, perhaps generated by some other part of the code or even generated in response to user interactions.

In our drawing app, we might let the user create a sequence of transformations and give it a name. That sequence could then be applied to shapes selected by the user.

Any time you find yourself with a bunch of repetitive code, see if you can extract the variable part from the part that stays the same, and move that variable part into a data structure.

Ponder	

The transformation example used a list of functions to drive the transformation loop. That means that the code that creates the list must be in the same scope as the functions themselves. But perhaps the transforms list is being constructed by one application and then interpreted by another.

How would you change the code to handle this?

Simplify Your Tests Using Tables

A few years back I wrote an assembler and emulator for the PDP-11, the most popular minicomputer of the 1970s. It was one of those systems where you just had to get it right. A subtle bug in instruction decoding and execution might not reveal itself until some code that the emulator was executing just happened to trigger it.

One set of tests made sure that the emulator could correctly identify which machine instruction it was about to execute. This wasn't as easy as it sounds—the PDP-11 instruction format was designed to fit as much information as possible into every 16-bit word. Sometimes one word would represent an opcode, two addressing modes, and two registers. Other times it might hold a branch instruction with a relative offset.

I needed hundreds of instruction decode tests. Here's one approach:

```
test(`decode mov`, () => {
  expect(emulator.decode(0o010000)).toBe(`mov`)
})
test(`decode movb`, () => {
  expect(emulator.decode(0o110000)).toBe(`movb`)
})
test(`decode cmp`, () => {
  expect(emulator.decode(0o020000)).toBe(`cmp`)
})
// and so on for page after page
```

This was a lot of repetitive copying and pasting. Even worse, all the boilerplate makes it hard to see the actual thing we're testing.

Table-driven code to the rescue:

```
([
  [ 0o010000, `mov` ],
  [ 0o110000, `movb` ],
  [ 0o020000, `cmp` ],
  //    :        :
  [ 0o160000, `sub` ],
]).forEach(([instruction, op]) => {
  test(`decode ${op}`, () => {
    expect(emulator.decode(instruction)).toBe(op)
  })
})
```

The table contains a sequence of test cases—each row contains a binary value representing the instruction along with the name of the corresponding opcode.

We iterate over the table, generating a unique test for each row. We embed the opcode name into the name of the test (to make it easier to see what's going on), and we verify that the decode is correct with the expect().toBe() assertion.

| Idea 48 | **Use tables to drive repetitive tests** |

Drive Multistep Tests with Data

Tables really shine when you're building more complex tests.

For example, Shopify has a wonderful, well-documented GraphQL API. I wanted to see if I could use it to feed order data into our royalty system.

The problem? The API can give you the current state of an order, but it doesn't tell you how it arrived in that state. A customer might buy something but not pay immediately, so the API would return an order with no payment transactions. Later, they complete the payment, so the API would give us the same order but with one or more payment transactions and perhaps some modified totals. Later on the customer discovers they could have used a coupon and asks the support staff if they could apply it to the order. Now the GQL contains three or four more records, showing discount information, discount applications, and refund transactions.

At our end, we have to reconcile the current state of an order with the last known state, determine what events have occurred, and then work out what it means in terms of the allocation of the money received with each title in the order.

Each test contained multiple steps.

1. We'd start with the first API response and verify we'd captured it correctly.

2. Then, in the same test (because we needed the prior state), we'd fetch the next response and check that we'd correctly interpreted the changes.

3. Repeat step 2 perhaps four or five times.

As always, the first test I coded by hand. It tested just a single API response and was about 135 lines long. The next test handled two responses and was well over 200 lines of code.

But now I could see the patterns and refactor out everything apart from the incoming data and the expected results. These values went into a table, and that table was the test.

The test data ended up looking something like this:

```
[ "three items then refund one", [
    [ ... step1 ... ],
    [ ... step2 ... ],
    [ ... step3 ... ],
]]
```

Each step was a nested table:

```
[
  "#2288-a-start-with-one-item",
  expect(2288, TEST_USER_FOX_HOLLOW, TEST_USER_FOX_HOLLOW) do
    {
        tax_total:      BigDecimal("2.06"),
        shipping_total: BigDecimal("0"),
        discount_total: BigDecimal("0"),
        grand_total:    BigDecimal("27.01"),
        product_total:  BigDecimal("24.95"),
        line_items:     [
                          [ "tvmelixir-p-00", 1, BigDecimal("24.95") ],
                        ],
        royalty_lines: [],
    }
  end
]
```

The first element of the list identified the fixture to load—this was a file containing a GraphQL message. The second element was a structure representing the expected state of the order after that message had been processed. Orders are complex, spread across half-a-dozen tables, so I created an expect helper that generated the boilerplate content and let me supply just the values I cared about.

All the code I'd written for the first test was still there. I'd just factored it out into something that would accept the fixtures and expected values from the table. When I needed a new test, I could concentrate on the inputs and outputs and not write any additional code. That simplicity encouraged me to test scenarios I might have glossed over if each test was a fresh 250-line method.

Tests Are Already Data Driven

For anything more than the most basic test, you're likely to create data structures representing the inputs to and the outputs from the code under test. In a way, we can say that the test that uses this data is already data-driven.

But if you have multiple tests that follow the same pattern—each with different inputs and outputs—you can extract the test logic into a function and parameterize it with a data table. Stick that data into a list and iterate over it, calling the test function for each row. Just make sure that if a test fails, it logs the data that caused that failure.

Not only does this make your tests easier to write and maintain, but it's also a great way to boost your test count statistics...

Explore	

You know what I'm going to suggest—have a look through the tests on some recent project. How many opportunities do you see to refactor parts of them into a data-driven style?

Practice 22

Simplify Logic with State Machines

Table-driven code is great for simplifying repetitive sequences of code. State machines take this to the next level by adding context and the ability to decide dynamically which code to run in a given situation.

(You may see state machines referred to as *finite state automata* or *finite state machines*.)

However, a lot of FUD is directed at state machines. As a result many developers avoid them. That's just plain silly—a simple state machine can make your code far easier to understand and change.

Idea 49	**You don't need libraries or design patterns to write a state machine**

I use state machines all the time, and each time they have improved the code I was working on. Here are a few examples:

Parsing
> I needed to parse a file that was *almost* in comma separated variable (CSV), but it used backslash to escape characters.

Extracting information from a Shopify order
> Shopify orders are complex beasts, with many record types and intricate rules. A state machine helped me make sure the correct information was presented in the right order.

Handling order fulfillment
> A simple state machine handled the changes in an order's fulfillment status, generating shipments, refunds, and notification as needed.

Detecting patterns in log messages
> I had to analyze web server log messages in real time, looking for times where a particular URL was accessed three times within five seconds from the same IP address. Many such patterns could overlap in the stream of messages. This turned out to be simple, using a set of dynamically generated state machines.

The list goes on.

Whenever you are handling a sequence of *events*, where each event affects how the next event should be handled, consider using a state machine. If these events are spread out over time, with potentially long delays between each, the case for using a state machine is even more compelling. They'll make your life simpler.

Implementing State Machines

You don't need complex libraries or long-winded pattern-based approaches when you need a state machine. All you need is a *lookup table*.

Let's start with a simple state machine—a push-button pen. Each time you press the button, the tip extends if it was retracted and retracts if it was extended.

A state machine is defined by *events*, *states*, and *transitions*. The machine sits in a particular state until an event comes along. This may cause a transition into a different state.

In the case of our retractable pen, we have the following:

- One event type—the button was pressed.
- Two states—extended and retracted.
- Two transitions—extended→retracted and retracted→extended.

If you click the top when the pen is extended, it transitions to being retracted, and if you click it when it's retracted, it transitions to extended.

We draw state machines with the states in boxes or circles and the transitions as arrows between states. The transitions are labeled with the event that triggers them.

Here's a state machine diagram that describes our retractable ball-point pen.

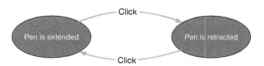

This is a simple diagram, but when they get more complicated, I like to see how they work by putting my finger on a state and then imagining an incoming event. I find the arrow labeled by that event, and my finger follows it to the next state.

What about the implementation? Well, this particular state machine is so simple that all we need is a Boolean:

```
let penRetracted = true

eventStream.on("click", () => {
  penRetracted = !penRetracted
}
```

It may not look like much, but that's a working state machine. Still, let's get a little more complicated.

A More Complicated Example: A Keypad Lock

Here's a keypad lock. It opens when you press $1 \rightarrow 5 \rightarrow 9$ in sequence.

- The user can press any number of keys before entering the correct sequence.
- If they enter a wrong digit, they must start over.
- If they enter 1 in the middle of a valid sequence, it should reset the sequence.

Try it

Before looking at the state diagram below, try sketching your own version. Use the finger technique to make sure it correctly unlocks given the sequences 159, 432159, 15159.

Here's my version of the state diagram:

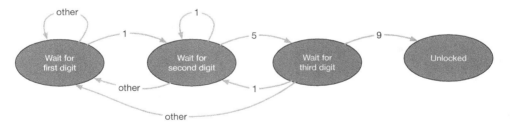

The trick is returning to the "wait for second digit" state if a 1 is pressed in the middle of what started as a valid sequence.

Implementing the Keypad Lock

To implement this, I'd use a lookup table (a dictionary, hash, map, or object, depending on your language). The code is on the next page.

```
fsm/159.rb
TRANSITIONS = {
  "wait_for_first_digit" => {
    "1"     => "wait_for_second_digit",
    "other" => "wait_for_first_digit",
  },

  "wait_for_second_digit" => {
    "5"     => "wait_for_third_digit",
    "1"     => "wait_for_second_digit",
    "other" => "wait_for_first_digit",

  },

  "wait_for_third_digit" => {
    "9"     => "unlocked",
    "1"     => "wait_for_second_digit",
    "other" => "wait_for_first_digit",
  },

  "unlocked" => NIL
}
```

The entire state transition logic is encapsulated in this data structure.

- Each state is a key in the dictionary.

- The values are nested maps that define what state to transition to based on incoming input.

The code that handles this is trivial:

```
fsm/159.rb
state = "wait_for_first_digit"
while TRANSITIONS[state] && key = gets()
  key   = key.strip
  state = TRANSITIONS[state][key] || TRANSITIONS[state]["other"]
end
```

In fact, the actual state machine implementation is just one line of code (it has the arrow in the margin).

But Wait, There's More

At this point I could dive deep into all the other cool things you can do with state machines. You can encode actions to take on each transition into the table. You can have long-running state machines, which persist their state between events. You can use state machines to drive workflows. And you can turn much of the stuff that happens inside your code into events, meaning you can use state machines to implement the logic of handling them.

But that's way too much detail for this book. If you're interested (of course you are), I have an article about it.[1]

∘∘⦿∘∘

The End of the Data Drive

Most of the chapters in this book don't have a summary like this. But I feel that this discussion of data and code is important enough to warrant it.

Over the years, I have come to appreciate the elegance and simplicity that is achievable when you find the right balance between code and the data that drives it. Too much code, and you lose flexibility. Too much data, and it can be hard to see what the code does.

But the sweet spot, when the data drives the code, and the code is decoupled from both the data and other code—that sweet spot is a magical place to be.

Please, start to experiment with driving your code with simple data structures. Start off gently. As you build an intuition, push yourself to use data more and more.

I'll be very surprised if you don't come to like where you end up.

Keep your eyes open for opportunities

Over the coming months, look for opportunities to transition to a more data-driven style. Here are a few things that you might come across:

- If you see repetitive stanzas of code that differ by a few values, perhaps make it list driven.
- Situations where a sequence of actions are taken, and that sequence changes depending on the circumstances, could be implemented as a simple interpreter.
- If you need to handle a stream of incoming events, and prior events affect the processing of the next, then look into state machines.

That list is just to seed your imagination. The more you look, the more you'll find ways to move logic out of code and simplify your life. *Carpe datum!*

---

1. https://articles.pragdave.me/p/simplify-logic-with-state-machines

## CHAPTER 8

Down at the Codeface

I don't care if you use two- or four-character indentation, whether you put the opening brace at the start of the next line, or any of the other ridiculous things developers argue about whenever code formatting comes up.

I care about two main things:

- Is it simple to read?
- Is it simple to edit?

Can I:

- Find things quickly?
- See the structure at a glance?
- Add and remove things with the minimum number of collateral updates?

Here I'm not talking about the design of the code; I'm talking about the source files, the program text—the stuff I see in an editor buffer.

The practices in this chapter are things *I* do to make *my* code easier for *me* to read and modify. But this is just *my* list.

Keep an eye on your own code. Are there patterns you use that make changes more difficult? Do you ever find yourself scanning a page of code, struggling to find what you need? If so, stop and ask yourself how you might make it clearer next time.

Practice 23

No Comment

Some developers write comments. Lots of comments. Excessive numbers of comments. Every file, every module, every function, every variable, and every parameter has a novella attached to it, with all the types annotated, the exceptions listed, and emergency contact information in case any of the naming is triggering.

> **Idea 50** **Make the code readable; cut back the comments**

As far as I'm concerned, this is a bad practice. First, it means that any change to the code involves twice as much work: change the code, and you have to make sure that you also update any related comment text. And, because comments aren't typically tested, there's no guarantee that those comment changes are correct. Over time, the comments become a net negative; they aren't accurate, so no one trusts them, and they're a boat anchor when it comes to making changes.

Some languages *do* have support for embedding tests in comments. Elixir, for example, supports embedding sample code snippets in comment blocks, along with the expected results. It can then extract these and run them as unit tests, ensuring that the code, when run, does in fact produce those results. Also available are libraries that add that functionality to other languages (Doctest-JS[1] for JavaScript, doctest[2] for Python, and so on).

I think there are three good reasons to add comments to code:

- You're using a tool that will extract them and create documentation. This is far and away the best way to document APIs and command-line tools.

- You need to tell a future reader of the code *why* you chose to do something in an unexpected way. For example, "We add the refund into the total because the API refund field is a negative number."

- To add #TODO and other flags (see the next practice).

---

1. https://github.com/supabase/doctest-js
2. https://docs.python.org/3/library/doctest.html

Actually, there's one more reason, and it's probably the one I use the most. I like to use comments to help clarify and break up the structure of my code. For example, this book is built from 50 or so markdown source files, controlled by a top-level manifest. That manifest file looks like this:

```
- part:    ########################
    title: Simplify Your Environment
           ########################
    intro-wide: |
       <imagedata alt="Octahedron, the third Platonic solid"
                  fileref="images/parts/octa.png" width="30%"/>
    include:
      - Automate
      - Research
- part:    #########################
    title: Simplify Your Interactions
           #########################
    intro-wide: |
       <imagedata alt="Dodecahedron, the fourth Platonic solid"
                  fileref="images/parts/dodeca.png" width="30%"/>
    include:
      - SoftSkills
```

I put comments around the names of the top-level parts just to make them stand out. I often put lines of stars between major sections of source code. When I'm feeling frisky, I'll use an editor plugin that draws comment boxes around function names.

We said it in *The Pragmatic Programmer, 20th Anniversary Edition [TH19]*, and I'll say it again. If your code needs comments for any other reason, the chances are it's the code's fault.

Part 1: Look for the commenting Goldilocks zone...

Too many comments are bad. No comments might be a little presumptuous in all but the simplest code. So find a level you're comfortable with.

Part 2: ...then cut them back

After a month or so of your new *minimal comment* regime, look back at your code. Are there any comments that describe how some code works? Delete them; the code should speak for itself. Did you find any comments describing what parameters to functions contained? Delete them and rename the parameters to make it clearer. Make each comment justify its existence, then thank it for its service.

Practice 24

TODO or Not TODO

When I'm heads-down writing code, I'll often realize that a change I'm making will affect another piece of code. Or perhaps while working on a change, I'll notice an unrelated bug in some adjacent code.

In the old days I'd head off, make those changes, then return to the original task. But when I get back, I've lost context; I have to spend some time rereading the code and repeating my initial analysis. Change is slow.

Now I do it differently. I look at the secondary change. If it's something like a simple typo or changing a parameter value, I'll do it then and continue working the original problem. For anything that's bigger, I now slap in a TODO comment.

```
shape = ellipse(r, r)      # TODO:: could this just be a circle?
#
# . . . code I'm actually changing
```

My editor highlights[3] these in the code (in fact, it even highlighted the previous code example as I typed it).

Neovim also has a handy-dandy project-wide summary of all TODO-type comments:

---

3.   https://github.com/folke/todo-comments.nvim

I discovered a secondary benefit of doing this. Not only do I get changes made faster, but I now have a list of small tasks I can use to fill in the five minutes before a meeting starts.

Find your editor's TODO functionality

I know that your editor will have something similar (a VS Code TODO highlighter plugin has over five million installs).

Line 'em Up

This Ruby program contains a list of countries in the European Union.

```ruby
COUNTRIES = ["Austria", "Belgium", "Bulgaria", "Croatia", "Republic of Cyprus",
"Czech Republic", "Denmark", "Estonia", "Finland", "France" "Germany",
"Greece", "Hungary", "Ireland", "Italy", "Latvia", "Lithuania", "Luxembourg",
"Malta", "Netherlands", "Poland", "Portugal", "Romania",
"Slovakia", "Slovenia", "Spain", "Sweden" ]

puts COUNTRIES.length    #=> 26
```

When we print the length of the list, we get 26, but there should be 27. How long does it take you to see the problem?

Here's the same list, formatted a little differently.

```ruby
COUNTRIES = [
  "Austria",    "Belgium",            "Bulgaria", "Croatia",
  "Cyprus",     "Czech Republic",     "Denmark",  "Estonia",
  "Finland",    "France" "Germany",   "Greece",
  "Hungary",    "Ireland",            "Italy",    "Latvia",
  "Lithuania", "Luxembourg",          "Malta",    "Netherlands",
  "Poland",     "Portugal",           "Romania",  "Slovakia",
  "Slovenia",   "Spain",              "Sweden"
]

puts COUNTRIES.length    #=> 26
```

See the problem now?

Here's another example of code that fails when run:

```ruby
weight = containerContents.weight
size = containerContent.size
items = contaierContent.items
```

Can you see two errors? How about now:

```ruby
weight = containerContents.weight
size   = containerContent.size
items  = contaierContent.items
```

The brain is incredibly good at seeing patterns. When things are lined up, anomalies jump out at us. I find that adding the occasional space to put things into columns finds an incredible number of stupid errors.

| Idea 51 | **Help your brain find errors by using decent layout** |

Practicalities

I wouldn't do this if my editor didn't handle aligning things with a couple of keystrokes. For example, I'm typing this chapter using Neovim. To align the previous example I selected the code (v a s) and then invoked the EasyAlign plugin, telling it to align the equals signs (g a =). I bet your editor has a plugin for this, too.

This kind of aligning can get out of hand when names are wildly different lengths:

```
name             = "Nshuti"
address          = "123 Some Street"
shipping_country = "Rwanda"
postal_code      = "12345"
date             = "2025/01/01"
```

I find this harder to read, as my eye can get lost scanning across. However, rather than abandoning the idea, I'll typically align like-sized lines together.

```
name    = "Nshuti"
date    = "2025/01/01"
address = "123 Some Street"

shipping_country = "Rwanda"
postal_code      = "12345"
```

Choose an alignment plugin for your editor

I don't use VS Code much, but I just checked, and it seems to have dozens of alignment plugins. I suspect the same is true for most editors. In my experience, it takes a while to find one that works the way you think, but once you find something you like, learn how to drive it.

Practice 26

Dangle That Comma

Talking about lists of things, here's a tip that can lead to some pretty serious arguments.

When you write a list of things, you separate each element with a delimiter character (often a comma):

```
[ 1, 2, 3 ]
```

Some languages (C, C#, C++, JavaScript, Python, and Ruby, to name a few) allow a delimiter after the last element of a list:

```
[ 1, 2, 3, ]      # still just three elements
```

Why does that little comma help make code easy to change? Let's imagine a list of the five largest lakes, ordered by size, starting with the largest:

```
BIG_LAKES = [
  "Caspian",
  "Superior",
  "Victoria",
  "Huron",
  "Michigan"
]
```

The customer changes their mind and wants the list in alphabetic order. No problem—you use your editor's *sort* feature:

```
BIG_LAKES = [
  "Caspian",
  "Huron",
  "Michigan"
  "Superior",   # syntax error
  "Victoria",
]
```

What was the last element is now in the middle, and it has no comma after it, so we get an error. With a trailing comma, however, the last element isn't special, and the list can be manipulated any way you'd like.

Practice 27

Sort 'em Out

If I'm typing in some kind of collection literal, and if the order of the items doesn't matter, then I'll sort the items.

For example, TypeScript has enumerated types:

```
enum Purple {
  Eggplant,
  Lavender,
  Lilac,
  Mauve,
  Rebecca,
  Royal,
  Violet,
}
```

I often use hashes (dictionaries) to pass in options. I sort the keys:

```
circle(
  fill: RED,
  stroke: BLACK,
  text: "push me",
  x_pos: 231,
  y_pos: 34,
)
```

This is also a good candidate for alignment.

```
circle(
  fill:    RED,
  stroke:  BLACK,
  text:    "push me",
  x_pos:   231,
  y_pos:   34,
)
```

You may never feel the need to use this technique. But, even so, look for times when you accidentally duplicate an item when adding it to an existing list or when you lose your place typing a list in. If it happens, perhaps give the sorting trick a go.

(This only applies if your editor lets you sort a selection of lines. I bet yours does...)

Tall Beats Wide

You youngsters have it easy. When I were a lad, we celebrated the switch from paper-roll teletypes to video terminals. Our screens were 80 characters wide (the number of columns on a punch card) and 24 lines high, green on black. And we loved it.

Now y'all have 56-inch 8K displays with pixels the size of atoms and a built-in coffee maker.

The trouble is some folks open an editor full screen and type code until it hits the right edge of the screen—200 characters, 300 characters, whatever fits.

Reading this code is a nightmare. Many studies have shown that the optimum line length when reading is between 45 to 75 characters. Much longer and your eye can get lost, forcing you to rescan the line from the beginning. And finding the beginning of that line can be tricky, too.

But line length is one of those things that start coffee-break arguments, so let's look at it a different way. Here's the same code, written two ways. First, compactly (sorry about the font size):

```
Product.find_by_sql [%{select distinct products.* from products, skus, author_sku_royalties where skus.product_id = products.id
  and author_sku_royalties.sku_id = skus.id and author_sku_royalties.user_id = ? order by products.title }, self.id]
```

And now formatted onto multiple lines:

```
Product.find_by_sql [%{
  select distinct products.*
    from products, skus, author_sku_royalties
  where skus.product_id = products.id
    and author_sku_royalties.sku_id = skus.id
    and author_sku_royalties.user_id = ?
  order by products.title
}, self.id]
```

Think about maintaining this code. Maybe you need to add a new table and the corresponding join clause. Clearly you can do it in either layout, but which makes it easier?

When we were punching our code on cards, making lines as long as possible reduced card count and the resulting back strain caused by carrying the card deck to the reader. You young whippersnappers don't have that issue. Enjoy the freedom and stack your code down the screen. And if you still want to use *all* your monitor, rotate it 90°.

Keep It Local

Back in college, I was taught that modularity and encapsulation were the keys to writing maintainable software—it's easier to change things if the impact of that change is bounded by the perimeter of a module. That's hard to argue with; software (or just about anything for that matter) would be impossible to work with if every change we made had a potentially global impact.

But, as with all things, breaking code into modules isn't always the right thing to do, at least from the start. Sometimes the simplest way to create something new is to break the rules.

Let's look at a Rails application as an example. Now, before I get started, I need to say that I'm not picking on Rails here: what I'm about to describe is pretty universal. It's just that I'm in the middle of converting a fairly large Rails site as I'm writing, so the issues are fresh in my mind.

The Good and Bad of Conventions

Rails (quite rightly) promises "convention over configuration." If you put stuff in the right place, with the right name, Rails will find and use it without the need for you to do any knitting. This can be a big time saver. It also means you can look at any Rails project and find your way around: they all look the same.

But, when followed slavishly, these conventions can actually make things more difficult to change, particularly during the early stages of a project. To illustrate this, let's look at a simple Rails view.

Anatomy of a View

By convention, Rails apps are organized around the idea of resources. Each resource will have a controller, a set of view templates, and most likely a model—it's an MVC framework. If we have a resource named customer, then the source code of the controller will be in app/controllers/customers_controller and the view templates will be in the directory app/views/customers. In addition, Rails looks for the file app/helpers/customers_helper.rb. The helpers are Ruby methods that you can call in any of the customer templates. Finally, your view might need some CSS and some JavaScript.

That's five files, widely spread across a directory tree. That's not a tragedy, but it does slow things down, particularly when you're first writing the code.

```
└── app
    ├── assets
    │   └── stylesheets
    │       └── customers.css
    ├──javascript
    │   └── controllers
    │       └── customers.js
    ├── controllers
    │   └── customers_controller.rb
    ├── helpers
    │   └── customers_helper.rb
    └── views
        └── customers
            └── show.html.erb
```

Here's what I do:

```
└── app
    ├── controllers
    │   └── customers_controller.rb
    └── views
        └── customers
            └── show.html.erb
```

Two files: the controller and the view template. The controller code is normally boilerplate, so most of my activity is in the template—that's where I put all my view code: CSS, JavaScript, helpers, and the template itself.

Here's what one of those templates looks like:

```
show.html.erb
<style>
  -- any view specific css
</style>

<script>
  // any local JavaScript
</script>

<%
  # any view helper functions (Ruby)
%>

<div>
  -- and the template itself
</div>
```

I start by fleshing out the template. When I find I need some code (often to do with formatting), I just add a function to the helper functions block in the same file. In the rare cases I also need to do some stylin', I add CSS to the top of the file.

Being able to work in one place without switching back and forth makes my life simple.

Should I find myself needing the same helper function in multiple views, I'll extract it into a normal xxx_helper.rb file. This doesn't affect the template.

I can hear some of you saying, "We *know* that's just wrong. You need to follow the conventions." Maybe you're right. But so far I've seen no ill effects. If I do, splitting the file will be easy.

I can also hear Elm and React developers saying, "You just realized this? We've been doing it all along." Indeed you have; indeed you have. And your success doing so helped convince me that this approach is viable, and not just for view components.

Splitting Regular Source Code

The "keep it local in one file" philosophy doesn't just apply to Rails views. I use it all the time.

When I'm writing some new code, I typically start out with a single file. I'll flesh out the outline, which will often involve creating new modules and classes. I'll just put them in that same file. As the code starts to take shape, I'll add more modules, again all in that one file. Why? Because it is so much simpler to refactor as I experiment with alternative structures. Moving code around, renaming things, and even just searching for things is easier.

When I get to the point where it's stable, I step back and look at the whole thing. I ask myself, When I come back to this in six months, how hard will it be to pick it back up when it's all one piece? Often I just leave it. But just as often I'll split it into separate source files, often in a subdirectory. In addition, the second I want to share functionality from that code to some other module, I'll likely split the code I'm sharing out into its own file. Doing so reduces the dependency footprint and therefore ties that other module to less of the original code.

Eating My Own Dog Food

As I was typing this section, I realized that I also apply this approach while writing. This book is written in Markdown. I know that I want a separate file for each chapter, because that way I can build the chapters independently. But initially that's the only structure I put in place. As with coding, I spend a lot of my time when writing moving stuff around, and having it all in one place really helps.

It's now a few months later. At some point, I must have needed to reorder the content at the individual practice level, so this chapter is now one top-level file and seven additional files in a subdirectory, each holding one practice. (And yes, that seven may well change…)

Be unconventional

Are you working in an environment where code is split across multiple files by convention? Would things break if you tried starting with everything in a single file?

Perhaps try it. If you're on a team and don't want them to beat you up about your radical code organization, just use the technique locally as you create new functionality. Then, before you push your changes, you can split your single file into many.

Along the way, see if the single-file solution makes things simpler. If so, perhaps mention it to your team, and see if they'd like to experiment, too.

Even if they don't, if the technique works for you, use it.

## CHAPTER 9

Outroduction

It's the end of the book, and I've managed to avoid the most difficult question: What is simplicity? Or, putting it another way, *How can I tell that one way of doing something is simpler than another?*

It's a difficult question because, as with many things in this book, the answer depends on the context. But there are some general things I look for when evaluating a possible path forward.

S is probably simpler than C if the following are true:

S is easier to understand than C

- Can I get an impression of what S does, and how it does it, faster than I can with C?
- Can I express what S does to someone else with simpler sentences than with C?
- Does S make me pause less often than C when I have to deconstruct some gnarly code or use an obscure library?
- Do I feel more confident that I could change S compared to C?

S has fewer parts than C

- Does S have fewer components, dependencies, rules, or conditions than C?
- Can S achieve the same outcome with fewer steps than C?

S reflects the problem more directly than C

- Does S more closely adhere to the idioms and language of the problem than C?
- Does C contain extra features, redundancy, or noise that S eliminates?

Simplicity is the essence of clarity, minimalism, and ease. It means stripping away the unnecessary to reveal what truly matters. In the design of physical things, it's about clean lines and intuitive function. In life, it's about focusing on what's meaningful and eliminating distractions. In code, it's all of these.

Simplicity is not simple—it's intentional, refined, and effective. It brings peace, efficiency, and elegance.

Simplicity is not absolute. What is simple to one person may not be to another. What is simple for someone might not have been simple for them last year.

Simplicity has no litmus test. It has no metrics; no rules.

Ultimately, something is simple *for me* if I feel good about it. Does it have that elusive *quality without a name*? Can I walk away from the keyboard without nagging doubts? Does it feel right?

I urge you to simplify your code, your coding, and possibly even your life. It will make you more productive and less stressed, and it will bring some enjoyment—some fun—back to your work.

You deserve that.

Dave

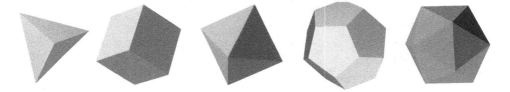

Bibliography

[AIS77]   Christopher Alexander, Sara Ishikawa, and Murray Silverstein. *A Pattern Language: Towns, Buildings, Construction.* Oxford University Press, New York, NY, 1977.

[Bec00]   Kent Beck. *Extreme Programming Explained: Embrace Change.* Addison-Wesley Longman, Boston, MA, 2000.

[de 97]   Gavin de Becker. *The Gift of Fear.* Little, Brown and Company, New York, NY, First edition, 1997.

[TH19]   David Thomas and Andrew Hunt. *The Pragmatic Programmer, 20th Anniversary Edition.* The Pragmatic Bookshelf, Dallas, TX, 2019.

Index

Thank you!

We hope you enjoyed this book and that you're already thinking about what you want to learn next. To help make that decision easier, we're offering you this gift.

Head on over to https://pragprog.com right now, and use the coupon code BUYANOTHER2025 to save 30% on your next ebook. Offer is void where prohibited or restricted. This offer does not apply to any edition of *The Pragmatic Programmer* ebook.

And if you'd like to share your own expertise with the world, why not propose a writing idea to us? After all, many of our best authors started off as our readers, just like you. With up to a 50% royalty, world-class editorial services, and a name you trust, there's nothing to lose. Visit https://pragprog.com/become-an-author/ today to learn more and to get started.

Thank you for your continued support. We hope to hear from you again soon!

The Pragmatic Bookshelf

SAVE 30%!
Use coupon code
BUYANOTHER2025

Agile Web Development with Rails 7.2

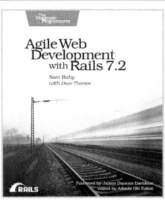

Rails 7.2 completely redefined what it means to produce fantastic user experiences and provides a way to achieve all the benefits of single-page applications—at a fraction of the complexity. Rails 7.2 integrated the Hotwire frameworks of Stimulus and Turbo directly as the new defaults, together with that hot newness of import maps. The result is a toolkit so powerful that it allows a single individual to create modern applications upon which they can build a competitive business. The way it used to be.

Sam Ruby
(472 pages) ISBN: 9798888651049. $67.95
https://pragprog.com/book/rails72

Programming Ruby 3.3 (5th Edition)

Ruby is one of the most important programming languages in use for web development. It powers the Rails framework, which is the backing of some of the most important sites on the web. The Pickaxe Book, named for the tool on the cover, is the definitive reference on Ruby, a highly-regarded, fully object-oriented programming language. This updated edition is a comprehensive reference on the language itself, with a tutorial on the most important features of Ruby—including pattern matching and Ractors—and describes the language through Ruby 3.3.

Noel Rappin, with Dave Thomas
(716 pages) ISBN: 9781680509823. $65.95
https://pragprog.com/book/ruby5

Programming Elixir 1.6

This book is *the* introduction to Elixir for experienced programmers, completely updated for Elixir 1.6 and beyond. Explore functional programming without the academic overtones (tell me about monads just one more time). Create concurrent applications, but get them right without all the locking and consistency headaches. Meet Elixir, a modern, functional, concurrent language built on the rock-solid Erlang VM. Elixir's pragmatic syntax and built-in support for metaprogramming will make you productive and keep you interested for the long haul. Maybe the time is right for the Next Big Thing. Maybe it's Elixir.

Dave Thomas
(410 pages) ISBN: 9781680502992. $47.95
https://pragprog.com/book/elixir16

Engineering Elixir Applications

The days of separate dev and ops teams are over—knowledge silos and the "throw it over the fence" culture they create are the enemy of progress. As an engineer or developer, you need to confidently own each stage of the software delivery process. This book introduces a new paradigm, *BEAMOps,* that helps you build, test, deploy, and debug BEAM applications. Create effective development and deployment strategies; leverage continuous improvement pipelines; and ensure environment integrity. Combine operational orchestrators such as Docker Swarm with the distribution, fault tolerance, and scalability of the BEAM, to create robust and reliable applications.

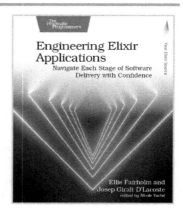

Ellie Fairholm and Josep Giralt D'Lacoste
(458 pages) ISBN: 9798888650677. $61.95
https://pragprog.com/book/beamops

Serverless Apps on Cloudflare

Use serverless technologies to build applications that scale, more quickly and easily, and without worrying about deployment. Whether you're writing an API, a full-stack app, or real-time code, harness the power of serverless on Cloudflare's platform so you can focus on what you do best: delivering solutions. With hands-on instruction and code samples throughout, you'll go from building a simple API to analyzing images with AI. And, when it's time to launch, you'll learn how to deploy your applications and websites automatically, and how to optimize their performance for production.

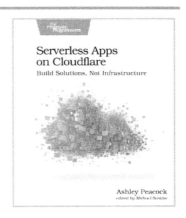

Ashley Peacock
(275 pages) ISBN: 9798888650714. $53.95
https://pragprog.com/book/apapps

Seven Obscure Languages in Seven Weeks

Explore seven older computer languages and discover new and fresh ideas that will change the way you think about programming. These languages were invented before we settled into our current C-style syntax and OO biases, so language designers were free to imagine what was possible. You'll find their insights thought-provoking, and their ideas will inspire you to try different (and possibly more productive) ways of programming. From a text manipulation language where every line is a potential state machine event, to a concurrent language where everything is done using actors, you're sure to come away from these seven languages inspired and excited.

Dmitry Zinoviev
(270 pages) ISBN: 9798888650639. $55.95
https://pragprog.com/book/dzseven

The Pragmatic Bookshelf

The Pragmatic Bookshelf features books written by professional developers for professional developers. The titles continue the well-known Pragmatic Programmer style and continue to garner awards and rave reviews. As development gets more and more difficult, the Pragmatic Programmers will be there with more titles and products to help you stay on top of your game.

Visit Us Online

This Book's Home Page
https://pragprog.com/book/dtcode
Source code from this book, errata, and other resources. Come give us feedback, too!

Keep Up-to-Date
https://pragprog.com
Join our announcement mailing list (low volume) or follow us on Twitter @pragprog for new titles, sales, coupons, hot tips, and more.

New and Noteworthy
https://pragprog.com/news
Check out the latest Pragmatic developments, new titles, and other offerings.

Save on the ebook

Save on the ebook versions of this title. Owning the paper version of this book entitles you to purchase the electronic versions at a terrific discount.

PDFs are great for carrying around on your laptop—they are hyperlinked, have color, and are fully searchable. Most titles are also available for the iPhone and iPod touch, Amazon Kindle, and other popular e-book readers.

Send a copy of your receipt to support@pragprog.com and we'll provide you with a discount coupon.

Contact Us

Online Orders:	*https://pragprog.com/catalog*
Customer Service:	*support@pragprog.com*
International Rights:	*translations@pragprog.com*
Academic Use:	*academic@pragprog.com*
Write for Us:	*http://write-for-us.pragprog.com*

www.ingramcontent.com/pod-product-compliance
Lightning Source LLC
La Vergne TN
LVHW081345050326
832903LV00024B/1319